For Grade
6

Read on Target

Using Reading Maps to Improve Reading Comprehension and to Increase Critical-Thinking Skills

Written By:
Sheila Anne Dean, M.S., CCC-SLP
Jeri Lynn Fox, M.S.
Pamela B. Meggyesy, M.A.
Pamela Marie Thompson, M.S.

Show What You Know® Publishing

Published By:
Show What You Know® Publishing
A Division of Englefield & Associates, Inc.
P.O. Box 341348
Columbus, OH 43234-1348
614-764-1211

www.showwhatyouknowpublishing.com

Printed in the United States of America
08 07 06   20 19 18 17 16 15 14 13 12 11 10 9 8 7 6 5 4 3 2 1

ISBN: 1-59230-152-5

About the Authors

Sheila Anne Dean, M.S., CCC-SLP, received a Bachelor's Degree from Ohio University and a Master's Degree from Miami University. She has worked for more than ten years in the public schools as a speech pathologist and a speech pathologist supervisor. Her role as a speech pathologist includes collaboration with teachers, parents, and other support staff while working with students individually, in small groups, and in the classroom setting. Previous presentations have included incorporating reading skills into therapy for school success, aligning instruction to meet classroom expectations, designing effective IEPs, and enhancing communication skills for at-risk and disabled children.

Jeri Lynn Fox, M.S., holds a Bachelor of Arts Degree from Bluffton College and a Master of Science Degree from the University of Dayton. A Martha Holden Jennings scholar, she has worked in public education for more than twenty-five years as a classroom teacher and school counselor. In her current role as school counselor, her responsibilities include improving student achievement, assessment coordination, and developing supportive parent/teacher partnerships and programming.

Pamela B. Meggyesy, M.A., earned a Bachelor of Science Degree in Education and a Master of Arts Degree in literature from Ohio University. Additionally, she has studied at Oxford University in Oxford, England. A thirty-year veteran classroom teacher in public schools, she has been involved with curriculum alignment and literature selection at the district and county levels. Additionally, she has chaired a district-wide writing initiative for her school system. She also has been an instructor at Wright State University.

Pamela Marie Thompson, M.S., has a Master's Degree in counseling from Wright State University and a Master's Degree in school psychology from the University of Dayton. She has taught at the college level and worked as a counselor and program director for a mental health clinic where she supervised case managers and a partial hospitalization program. She is currently employed as a school psychologist. Her background includes experience in testing, assessment, and academic intervention. She has worked in this field for eighteen years. An often sought-after speaker, she has presented numerous workshops dealing with a variety of educational topics including program evaluation, reading comprehension skill development, behavioral interventions, problem-solving skills, and instructional planning for the inclusive classroom. She has been a presenter for the Ohio School Psychologists Association state conference, the Association of School Administrators in Washington State, and the International Reading Association.

The authors have worked together for more than a decade in the Northridge School District in Dayton, Ohio. Their varied educational backgrounds and experiences bring a multifaceted approach to their collaborative educational projects.

Acknowledgements

Show What You Know® Publishing acknowledges the following for their efforts in making this assessment material available for students, parents, and teachers.

Cindi Englefield, President/Publisher
Eloise Boehm-Sasala, Vice President/Managing Editor
Lainie Burke Rosenthal, Project Editor/Graphic Designer
Erin McDonald, Project Editor
Christine Filippetti, Project Editor
Jill Borish, Project Editor
Charles V. Jackson, Project Editor
Heather Holliday, Project Editor
Jennifer Harney, Illustrator/Cover Designer

Dedication

To our families:

David, Sarah, Marie, Elaine, and Erin, thanks for your love.
Because of you, I truly "enjoy every day." –SAD

Richard, Amy, and Anna, thank you for the joy you bring to my life. –JLF

Joe, Mark, and Lauren; I treasure each of you. –PBM

Nathan, Olivia, and Jason, thanks for your love and encouragement. –PMT

and

To our first teachers:
our parents, by birth and by marriage,
with love and appreciation:

George and Carolyn Harrington and Carl and Marianna Dean –SAD

Charles and Edith Harlow and Richard and Janice Fox –JLF

George and Connie Besuden –PBM

Joe and Emily and Harold and Marie –PMT

Table of Contents

Chapter 1: Introduction 1

Chapter 2: Critical-Thinking Skills 3

   What? 3

   Why? 4

   How? 4

Chapter 3: Designing Instruction 7

   The Process 7

   Instructional Considerations 8

   Sample Lesson 10

Chapter 4: Reading Map Activities 13

   Activity 1: Analyze Aspects of the Text by Examining Characters 14

      Student Activity 1 15

   Activity 2: Analyze Aspects of the Text by Examining Setting 19

      Student Activity 2 20

   Activity 3: Analyze Aspects of the Text by Examining Plot 24

      Student Activity 3 25

   Activity 4: Analyze Aspects of the Text by Examining Problem/Solution 29

      Student Activity 4 30

   Activity 5: Analyze Aspects of the Text by Examining Point of View 34

      Student Activity 5 35

   Activity 6: Analyze Aspects of the Text by Examining Theme 39

      Student Activity 6 40

Activity 7: Infer from the Text 44

    Student Activity 7a 45

    Student Activity 7b 47

Activity 8: Predict from the Text 51

    Student Activity 8a 53

    Student Activity 8b 55

Activity 9: Compare and Contrast.. 59

    Student Activity 9a 60

    Student Activity 9b 62

Activity 10: Analyze the Text by Examining the Use of Fact and Opinion 66

    Student Activity 10a 68

    Student Activity 10b 71

Activity 11: Explain How and Why an Author Uses Contents of a Text
    to Support His/Her Purpose for Writing 76

    Student Activity 11a 77

    Student Activity 11b 79

Activity 12: Evaluate and Critique the Text for Organizational Structure 83

    Student Activity 12a 84

    Student Activity 12b 86

Activity 13: Evaluate and Critique the Text for Logic and Reasoning 91

    Student Activity 13a 92

    Student Activity 13b 94

Activity 14: Evaluate and Critique the Text 98

    Student Activity 14a 99

    Student Activity 14b 101

Activity 15: Summarize the Text 105

    Student Activity 15a 106

    Student Activity 15b 110

Activity 16: Identify Cause and Effect 115

    Student Activity 16a 116

    Student Activity 16b 118

    Student Activity 16c 121

Chapter 5: Conclusion 125

    Additional Resources 126

    Student Self-Scoring Chart 130

Chapter 1:
Introduction

Introduction

Read on Target is a comprehensive resource for parents, teachers, and students to address critical-thinking skills necessary for reading comprehension. It provides a well-developed, systematic approach to teach these skills. Included in the Parent/Teacher Edition are: teacher tip pages, troubleshooting sections, sample texts, reading maps (graphic organizers), and a 9-step instructional design process for parents and teachers to use. In addition, *Read on Target* provides a 4-step sequential process for students to use to understand and to complete the process of thinking critically.

A Student Workbook, sold separately, correlates with this Parent/Teacher Edition. This Student Workbook includes a 4-step process for student use. It includes sample texts, student tips, reading maps (graphic organizers), and critical-thinking questions relating to the specific critical-thinking skill. The graphic organizers are written in the form of reading maps. These reading maps are designed to supplement any reading comprehension program. They can be used to provide opportunities for students to practice critical-thinking skills related to reading comprehension. Sixteen reading maps are included to reflect the requirements for using critical-thinking skills.

Reading maps guide students through the thinking process and provide a blueprint from which to build their ideas into a clear, conceptual structure. Students can use the reading maps to make associations from the reading material and follow the steps to answer the questions. Then they can build their responses to match the requirements of each critical-thinking element. Students will be able to channel their ideas and thoughts to allow them to understand the implications of the question and enable them to deal with it clearly.

Reading maps are visual tools for students to use when answering critical-thinking questions. Students often want to skip organizational steps and leap immediately into answering questions without thinking about what they are being asked or required to answer. Reading maps focus on the steps to follow (the process of critical thinking) that are becoming a part of reading-comprehension tests in school and critical-thinking expectations in the work world. When reading maps are used daily, students develop consistency in the way they process and answer critical-thinking questions. They begin to understand the expectations and requirements of this process and are eventually able to make this process a part of their tools for success in life.

Today's high-stakes tests require students to respond to questions that demand the use of critical-thinking skills. *Read on Target* promotes student success on assessment outcomes for reading. These outcomes measure students' abilities to comprehend fiction, poetry, and nonfiction. The use of critical-thinking skills when answering multiple-choice and open-ended questions is essential in order for students to succeed.

Reading maps are designed to supplement curricular material for classroom instruction with grade 6. The reading maps can be used as guides during class, small-group, or individual instruction. The reading maps can be presented in any order and can be adapted as necessary for instructional purposes.

Information regarding the design of instruction that moves children from basic-content responses to higher-order-thinking responses is presented in Chapter 3. The reading maps included move students in a step-by-step approach that focuses on thinking critically in all content areas. Thus, instruction will be targeted to develop and to support critical-thinking skills through the use of reading maps to help students successfully organize necessary information.

When compared to actual curricular material, *Read on Target* provides students and teachers with sample texts containing easier readability levels. The sample texts have common, easy-to-read vocabulary and simple sentence structure. Thus, students will be able to center on the thought process rather than the decoding.

In addition, the authors' intent was to allow parents and teachers the opportunity to teach each critical-thinking skill in an organized, systematic way without requiring instruction on decoding skills. As students become more proficient in answering questions using critical-thinking skills, teachers and parents may add more challenging sample texts. Ultimately, the students will demonstrate success by answering questions using critical-thinking skills while simultaneously reading appropriate curricular material.

To help monitor student development, a rubric (check sheet) has been included at the end of the book. This will allow the instructor and the student to gauge student understanding of each critical-thinking skill. Used as self-assessments, the rubrics are essential for students' participation in tracking and understanding their own progress. When students self-assess, they learn to take ownership in managing their improvement. Using reading maps and rubrics will allow parents, teachers, and students to measure progress toward the critical-thinking standards required on today's state and national tests.

                                 © 2006 Englefield & Associates, Inc.

Chapter 2:
Critical-Thinking Skills

Critical-Thinking Skills

Teachers are expected to teach specific critical-thinking skills embedded in their curriculum. Definitions of **what** critical-thinking skills are, **why** critical-thinking skills are necessary, and **how** to teach these skills will enhance understanding of the instructional process.

What?

Critical-thinking skills for reading comprehension are the ability to reason and the ability to understand the meaning of what is read. Without critical-thinking skills, students cannot draw meaning from text. The purpose of critical thinking is to move beyond reading the content to a higher level of processing information. Developing effective reading skills includes understanding that critical thinking means reading for a purpose. These skills include breaking down information into parts and showing the relationship between them in order to understand the information. They also include the ability to reason, to differentiate between fact and opinion, to interpret information, to infer, and to predict from information drawn from knowledge and clues.

Specific critical-thinking skills addressed in the *Read on Target* book are as follows:

1. Analyze aspects of the text by examining the characters.

2. Analyze aspects of the text by examining the setting.

3. Analyze aspects of the text by examining the plot.

4. Analyze aspects of the text by examining the problem/solution.

5. Analyze aspects of the text by examining the point of view.

6. Analyze aspects of the text by examining the theme.

7. Infer from the text.

8. Predict from the text.

9. Compare and contrast.

10. Analyze the text by examining the use of fact and opinion.

11. Explain how and why the author uses contents of a text to support his/her purpose for writing.

12. Evaluate and critique the text for organizational structure.

13. Evaluate and critique the text for logic and reasoning.

14. Evaluate and critique the text.

15. Summarize the text.

16. Identify cause and effect.

Why?

In this age of achievement testing and educational accountability, students must be able to do more than restate facts. Increasingly, students are evaluated on their ability to read and to employ critical-thinking skills. Additionally, this ability is essential for success as an adult. Critical-thinking skills are used beyond the classroom—at home, at work, and in the community.

Mastery of critical-thinking skills develops the student's ability to function independently. Just as a parent teaches inferencing skills to the young child (for example, cueing the child to observe that it is cold and raining outdoors so he or she will choose appropriate outdoor clothes), the process of reading using critical-thinking skills can be directly taught. Students need more than cursory exposure to the development of these skills. Reading maps help students become successful critical thinkers in all content areas by breaking down the sequential embedded skills needed. For example, if a question includes the word "explain," students need to understand that the embedded vocabulary includes tell how (the process) or why (the reason). If students are asked to analyze, they are required to identify, list, describe, and determine the impact of the attributes. Thus, specific, direct sequential steps are required to complete a critical-thinking task.

Teaching children to read critically can be accomplished and mastered with practice and repetition. Critical-thinking skills enhance the ability to reason, to view information in divergent ways, and to solve problems. Additionally, these skills lead to creative and innovative ways to think about information. As children learn the process of thinking critically, they will be able to apply this process in real-life experiences. As adults, they will be able to use these same skills in the workplace and at home.

How?

Student success is the goal of every teacher in every classroom and is contingent upon teacher involvement and student performance. Teachers and parents strive to challenge students in all subject areas with innovative approaches to instruction, which is usually accomplished through a variety of tasks requiring students to read text and to comprehend materials they have read. Teachers and parents give instruction, monitor student progress, and encourage success using a question-and-answer format. Questions reflect varying levels of difficulty and often require the use of critical-thinking skills. Teaching students how to think critically is a process that can be directly taught. The reading maps included in *Read on Target* will guide students to understand the components of each specific skill.

It is important that teachers and parents understand the integral components of critical-thinking skills and their relationship to reading comprehension. They can then better tailor instruction and assessment to meet individual student needs. When students show weaknesses in critical-thinking skills, teachers and parents need to be equipped to modify the instructional format. The relationship between reading comprehension and critical thinking is evident as teachers and parents assess student knowledge through questions and answers. It is important to identify what is required for successful reading comprehension in order to understand the implications when responding to critical-thinking questions. Using reading maps allows teachers and parents to see the student's inability to understand the steps required for answering critical-thinking questions.

Difficulties occur when there is no immediate feedback to clarify what has been read. Unlike when participating in conversation, a student reading a passage has no opportunity to communicate with the author. Thus, when reading to think critically, it is important to have tools, such as reading maps, which provide a method for immediate understanding and clarification.

Reading maps provide students with the ability to repair or "fix" problems when they occur. Reading maps prompt the student to include all the necessary information for accurate, complete answers. In addition, students are guided through the steps inherent to each individual critical-thinking skill. To help students comprehend the text, instructors must be aware of the parts of the comprehension process. This process includes understanding the purpose of the question, having adequate vocabulary skills to accomplish the task, and accessing previous experiences and prior knowledge.

Understanding the purpose of the question allows the student to tap into what is expected in the response. The student will then know what specific elements are required. For example, if students are asked to evaluate, they are required to determine strengths and weaknesses of the text.

To comprehend the text, the student must understand that critical thinking is dependent on associated vocabulary. Students with weaker vocabularies have difficulty thinking critically about the text. When students do not know the meanings of key words, they are unable to answer questions requiring skills such as analyzing, predicting, inferring, comparing, and contrasting.

Another component of comprehension is remembering previous experiences. This enables students to use those experiences to make inferences about the text. If the students are presented with a text that mentions a "cold, snowy day," they will be able to infer that the character needs mittens and a hat because they themselves have needed mittens and a hat on a cold, snowy day.

Prior knowledge is also an important component for critical-thinking skills. Consider a text that includes information regarding a storm coming later in the day. The student is able to predict what the character may need to take before leaving the house. This prior knowledge of storms enables students to make predictions from the text. When students lack prior knowledge, they are less able to successfully answer questions requiring critical-thinking skills because they lack the broad knowledge base from which to build their answers.

It is important for teachers and parents to fully understand the features associated with critical-thinking skills. To achieve academic success, students need to demonstrate an ability to use critical-thinking skills and relate them to reading comprehension. Competency is therefore dependent upon the following elements: an understanding of the purpose of the critical-thinking question, adequate vocabulary skills, previous experiences, and sufficient prior knowledge.

Read on Target is a tool for teachers and parents to enhance instruction and to encourage success for reading comprehension. *Read on Target* is a must for all teachers and parents searching for a way to teach their students how to respond to questions requiring critical-thinking skills.

Chapter 3:
Designing Instruction

The Process

Teaching reading comprehension involves designing instruction that moves students from responding with basic facts to critical thinking about what is read. The process of designing instruction by following these sequential activities is as follows.

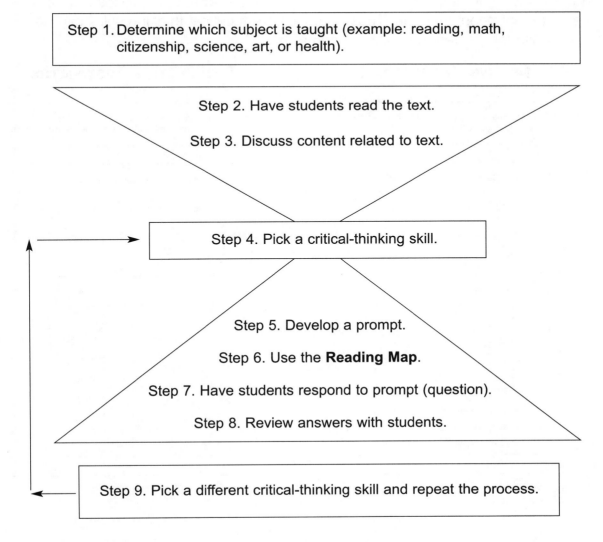

Step 1. Determine which subject is taught (example: reading, math, citizenship, science, art, or health).

Step 2. Have students read the text.

Step 3. Discuss content related to text.

Step 4. Pick a critical-thinking skill.

Step 5. Develop a prompt.

Step 6. Use the **Reading Map**.

Step 7. Have students respond to prompt (question).

Step 8. Review answers with students.

Step 9. Pick a different critical-thinking skill and repeat the process.

Instructional Considerations

Educators frequently experiment with new, creative approaches to improve instruction. Most often, teachers are successful in teaching the content for a particular subject; in fact, many statewide tests indicate teachers are very successful in teaching the content material. However, when content becomes more complicated by the addition of critical-thinking skill questions, students fail to achieve the same positive results because the instruction itself needs to be more focused and exact in eliciting higher-level thinking. We need to work toward more effective instruction in this area.

One effective way to improve instruction is to use a multilevel approach, such as in the illustration labeled "Effective Instruction." Essentially, teachers already have curriculum with key objectives and subject material they are expected to teach. They relay the information for a particular subject using a broad perspective. The discussion should center on the content of the text with critical-thinking skills incorporated into instruction using reading maps.

Students respond to questions and review answers with their teachers/parents as guides. Using a different skill, the student and teacher repeat the process. Note, the content has not been changed. Thus, many different critical-thinking skills can be utilized, while the content remains the same.

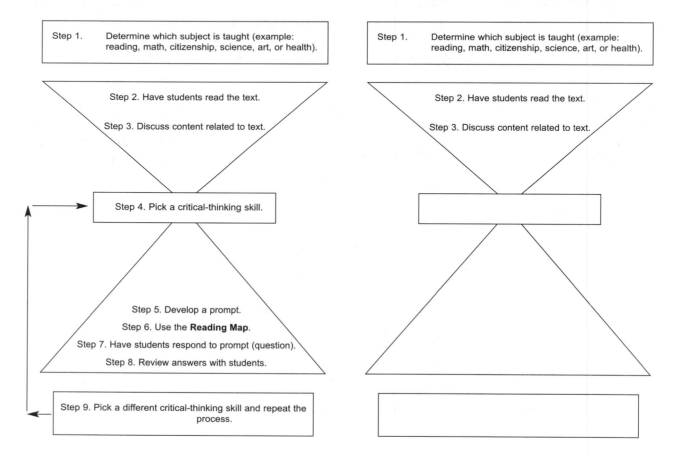

Effective Instruction   Ineffective Instruction

Step 1.   Determine which subject is taught (example: reading, math, citizenship, science, art, or health).

Step 2. Have students read the text.

Step 3. Discuss content related to text.

Step 4. Pick a critical-thinking skill.

Step 5. Develop a prompt.
Step 6. Use the **Reading Map**.
Step 7. Have students respond to prompt (question).
Step 8. Review answers with students.

Step 9. Pick a different critical-thinking skill and repeat the process.

The teacher-student learning gap typically occurs as teachers incorporate critical-thinking skills (see Chapter 2 for a complete list). Teachers expect the student to respond correctly without practice, repetition, or familiarity with which to answer that specific critical-thinking skill. When teachers realize students have difficulty responding appropriately to a specific question, they need to change instruction to meet the students' needs.

Referring to the connected yet inverted triangles in the illustration titled "Ineffective Instruction," students fail when teaching proceeds from reading the text material directly to discussing and testing the content. In this way, instruction does not permit the students to achieve total success. Success is not entirely achieved because Steps 4 thru 9 have not been included. Thus, students are not provided opportunities to practice critical thinking, as these skills are not directly taught.

When the steps crucial for successful instruction (Steps 4-9) are omitted, including targeting instruction to meet the critical-thinking skill and using a reading map for successful organization of necessary information, students fail to understand the components of critical thinking. "Effective Instruction" shows how to include a specific prompt and a corresponding reading map into the instructional process. For the student to respond accurately, teachers need to select which critical-thinking skill is difficult for the student. Specific prompts need to be developed that correspond to the subject material while simultaneously addressing critical-thinking skills. Effective instruction includes using these prompts in combination with a visual picture in the form of reading maps to guide students to understand the process of critical thinking.

By using the same content from the text, the teacher has the ability and the control to teach directly the critical-thinking skills necessary for successful reading comprehension. Simply, the teacher selects specific critical-thinking skills, develops appropriate prompts (questions) based upon the subject content, and provides students with the blueprint (reading map) for successfully responding to the question. Ultimately, the student achieves success, and the teacher meets individual needs while developing critical-thinking skills using curricular content.

Sample Lesson

This sample lesson was developed using the information and instructional design from the illustration labeled "Effective Instruction" on page 8.

Step 1.   Determine subject: Reading.

Step 2.   Students read text.

Sample Text:

One warm summer day, a mother worked in the house while her children played in the yard. The swings swayed with the breeze, and the sandbox lay open as the direct sunlight warmed the sand. Sarah, the oldest child, collected pinecones. Marie, the next oldest, lined up rocks on the patio. Elaine found acorns and sticks hidden toward the rear of the yard, as the baby, Erin, slept in a stroller on the sidewalk.

Around noon, the mother walked into the kitchen and opened the refrigerator door. Cool air gently brushed her face as she reached in to find the sliced turkey, lettuce, and cheese. She thought the apples looked good, and she washed some grapes, too.

After the mother had arranged all the necessary items, including the bread, she called the children to come inside the house.

Step 3.   Discuss text content. For example, the instructor asks students questions such as, "Who was in the kitchen?" and "What did she take out of the refrigerator?"

Step 4.   Pick a critical-thinking skill. For example, the instructor picks "Predicting."

Step 5.   Develop a prompt or a question to engage students. The instructor provides the predicting question, "What do you think the mother will have the children do when they come in from outside?"

                   © 2006 Englefield & Associates, Inc.

Step 6.   Use the reading map during guided and independent seat work.

To achieve success with writing in response to particular prompts, specifically designed reading maps provide students with the necessary framework. Reading maps and graphic organizers are tools used to help the student organize information by providing the student with a method for planning the written response. Reading maps are used for a variety of purposes and assist students to answer higher-level thinking questions.

Instruction for using reading maps should include the following sequence.

- Tell How

- Show How

- Help How

- Watch How

During the "Tell How" step of this sequence, the parent or teacher introduces the targeted critical-thinking skill and discusses the importance of this particular critical-thinking skill. The parent or teacher defines the skill and explains where the students may encounter this skill in subject areas as well as opportunities outside of school.

The "Show How" portion involves demonstrating for students exactly how the instructor determined the answer. The parent or teacher uses the students' background knowledge and adds new information taken from the selection. Using a specific reading map, the parent or teacher determines what information is important and demonstrates where the information is placed on the reading map tailored for the targeted skill.

"Help How" is actually guided practice for students. The students read a prompt developed specifically to improve a particular critical-thinking skill. The students are encouraged to use background knowledge and new information while completing the corresponding reading map. Instructors assist students as needed during this step. Some students require more direct involvement whereas others will succeed independently.

It is during the last part of the sequence, "Watch How," that instructors actually provide students with a reading task for independent work in order to expect student success. Sometimes, students continue to require reading maps during the final step. Students become familiar with the expectations of the reading map and feel comfortable with the ease with which their reading is organized. The students gain confidence and experience through the use of reading maps designed for specific reading tasks.

Step 7. **Students respond to the prompt/question in writing or orally.**

Step 8. **Review answers.**

Step 9. **Change the critical-thinking skill.** For example, the instructor selects "Analyze the Setting."

Using the same sample text from Step 2:

One warm summer day, a mother worked in the house while her children played in the yard. The swings swayed with the breeze, and the sandbox lay open as the direct sunlight warmed the sand. Sarah, the oldest child, collected pinecones. Marie, the next oldest, lined up rocks on the patio. Elaine found acorns and sticks hidden toward the rear of the yard, as the baby, Erin, slept in a stroller on the sidewalk.

Around noon, the mother walked into the kitchen and opened the refrigerator door. Cool air gently brushed her face as she reached in to find the sliced turkey, lettuce, and cheese. She thought the apples looked good, and she washed some grapes, too.

After the mother had arranged all the necessary items, including the bread, she called the children to come inside the house.

The prompt becomes, "If the setting is changed to a campground, how would the story be different?"

Using another critical-thinking skill, analyze the characters, the prompt becomes, "If the children were 15 years old, how would the story be different?" To use the fact and opinion critical-thinking skill, the prompt/question could resemble, "Is it true that the children enjoy playing outside?"

By using the same content from the text, the instructor has the ability and the control to teach directly specific critical-thinking skills necessary for successful reading comprehension. Simply, the instructor selects specific critical-thinking skills, develops appropriate prompts based upon the subject content, and provides students with the blueprint (reading map) for successful completion. Ultimately, the student achieves success, and the instructor meets individual needs while developing critical-thinking skills using curricular content.

 © 2006 Englefield & Associates, Inc.

Chapter 4:
Reading Map Activities

The contents of the *Read on Target for Grade 6, Student Workbook*, are found throughout Chapter Four.

There are 27 activities. Each Student Workbook activity includes:

- a sample text (Step 1),
- student tips (Step 2),
- reading maps (Step 3), and
- critical-thinking questions (Step 4).

In addition to Steps 1–4 from the Student Workbook, this Parent/Teacher Edition introduces each skill with Teaching Tips. Additionally, each skill closes with a Troubleshooting section. Sample responses for the reading maps and the critical-thinking questions are italicized. These responses are not included with the Student Workbook. They are for parent/teacher reference. The sample responses do not represent definitive answers. Rather, they are available for use as a guide. More than one answer may be correct.

Analyze Aspects of the Text
by Examining Characters

Teaching Tips

What Do Students Need to Know?

It is important to understand the characters when reading. Characters can be people, animals, or objects. Understanding characters goes beyond naming the character. Characters come alive by describing and identifying what they are like. Students need to develop a deeper understanding of characters by identifying their traits and attributes and considering the impact a character has on the story. Encourage your students to consider what the character does and why. They need to understand the embedded requirements of analyzing characters. These requirements include the ability to identify, to name, and to describe the characteristics and actions of the character. Next, students need to be able to look at each separate characteristic or action and think about the impact it has on the story. Finally, they need to consider how the story would be different if one of the characteristics or actions of the character changed.

Use of the Reading Maps

To analyze characters, consider their feelings, actions, and emotions. Students get to know the characters by reading what they say and do and how others react to them. By completing this reading map, students will practice skills that go beyond naming the character to obtain a deeper level of understanding of the character. The reading map will guide students to:

- Match a description of the character's attributes with a sentence from the story that tells about the character.

- Recognize that most of the descriptions listed on the reading map will be found in the story. The student should cross out any descriptions not found in the story.

- Tell how the story would change if the characters were different.

- Tell how the characters affected the story.

Activity 1

Smythe would feel better after reading the card. Of course, the teacher smiled when she saw the card. "What a nice surprise! Thank you so much, Olivia," said the teacher.

"You're welcome," Olivia replied shyly.

When Olivia returned to her seat, her pen fell out of her desk to the floor without her noticing. Ann picked it up and said, "Oh, this is my pen. I am so glad I found it." Ann mistakenly thought the pen was hers. Olivia did not say anything because she knew she had plenty more pens and was happy to let Ann keep that one. But during recess, Ann found Olivia and said, "I think this is your pen. I thought it was my pen, but after looking closer, I see it is yours."

Olivia replied, "Oh, thank you, but please just keep it as my gift to you." Ann was so happy to have this gift and thought Olivia was a good friend. She planned to share her art supplies with Olivia and her classmates during the art class.

The bell ending recess rang. Olivia and her friends went inside, as it was time for art class. "My favorite class!" exclaimed Olivia. She was even more excited when she saw how many different projects the children could choose to do. Olivia chose "Art and the Environment." Her teacher said they would plant acorns and try to grow an oak tree. Olivia smiled and said she would like that. Next, Olivia and her friends went outside and planted several acorns in the front schoolyard. They all hoped these would grow into big, beautiful oak trees someday. The children drew pictures of the small acorns and the trees that the acorns would someday grow to be. Olivia shared her pens and paper with her friends. They laughed and talked while they drew beautiful pictures. Olivia thought she was lucky to be able to share such a wonderful day with such good friends.

After school, Olivia and her friends talked about their day. They planned to check in the spring to see whether the acorns had grown into trees. Sure enough, that spring, Olivia came into the classroom and happily announced she had something to show everyone out in the schoolyard. The class was delighted to see some tiny sprouts coming up though the soil where they had planted the acorns. "These tiny sprouts should grow into big, beautiful trees," said Olivia. Her classmates brought out their art supplies and drew pictures of the sprouts. Everyone shared supplies.

Each year the baby oak trees grew larger and larger. Today, when Olivia brings her friends and family to the schoolyard, she tells them about when she and her friends planted the acorns. To this day, she has saved her art drawings of the acorns and the oak trees. She loves to look at them because they remind her of her friends and their fun activities in school.

Activity 1

Analyze Aspects of the Text by Examining Characters

I read to figure out what the characters are like. I get to know them.

Step 1 Read the story "Friends."

Friends

It was a crisp fall day the first week in October. Olivia woke up, got dressed, brushed her hair, and came down to breakfast. Olivia always had a sunshiny smile that seemed to match her bright, yellow hair. She knew today was an extra special day because it was the day of the traveling art class. She was excited as she explained to her family that the art museum teachers were coming to her school. There would be drawing, painting, and lots of outside activities, too. Olivia smiled as she told her family about the art class where they would be able to draw and make art projects. She thought everyone in the class would just love this activity. Hurriedly, she finished her breakfast and went to school.

On the way to school, Olivia saw her friends Sally and Ann walking to school. Olivia told her friends she loved school, especially anything that had to do with drawing, and she had decided to bring her special pens and pink paper for drawing. She thought it would be a good idea to bring extra supplies so she could share with her friends.

Sally said, "I just love those pens and the pink paper. It will be fun to draw with them at school. That was really nice of you."

Olivia replied, "I brought 15 pens so all of my friends will have something to use during recess and art class." As the girls continued, Olivia saw more of her friends walking to school. She invited them to walk with Sally, Ann, and her. They talked excitedly about the upcoming art class.

Upon arriving at school, Olivia put her special pens and paper in the desk. She noticed her teacher had a sprained wrist. She felt very bad for her teacher, as she knew how painful a sprained wrist could be. Olivia drew a beautiful "Get Well Soon" card and quietly placed it on her teacher's desk. She hoped Mrs.

Read on Target for Grade 6

Map 1.1	Analyze Aspects of the Text by Examining the Characters

I read to figure out what the characters are like. I get to know them.

Character's Name: _Olivia_

Describe the character.	Write a sentence from the story that tells about the character.	What does this tell you about the character?
What does the character look like?	*Olivia always had a sunshiny smile that seemed to match her bright yellow hair.*	*Olivia is cheerful and friendly.*
How does the character act?	*Olivia smiled as she told her family about art class. She shared pens and paper with her friends. She chose "Art and the Environment."*	*Olivia likes art class. Olivia is a caring, happy person.*
How does the character feel or think?	*Olivia thought it would be a good idea to bring extra supplies to share with her friends. She felt very bad for her teacher, as she knew how painful a sprained wrist could be.*	*Olivia is thoughtful and sympathetic.*
What does the character say?	*"I brought 15 pens so all my friends will have something to use during recess." "Please keep it as my gift to you," Olivia replied.*	*Olivia shares and wants to be a good friend.*
What good or bad thing is the character doing?	*Olivia drew a beautiful get well card and quietly placed it on her teacher's desk.*	*Olivia is good at drawing. She is kind. Olivia doesn't draw attention to her kind deeds.*
How do others react to the character?	*They laughed and talked while they drew beautiful pictures.*	*People like Olivia.*

Activity 1

© 2006 Englefield & Associates, Inc.

COPYING IS PROHIBITED

4

Note: Student answers may vary. Example responses in italics are for use as a guide.

Activity 1

Read on Target for Grade 6

Step 2

Student Tips

To analyze a character you need to remember:

- A character can be a person, an animal, or an object.
- What the character is like, because this affects the story.
- The story could change if you change one part of a character.

Step 3

Complete the reading maps. Use the reading maps to help you think about the character.

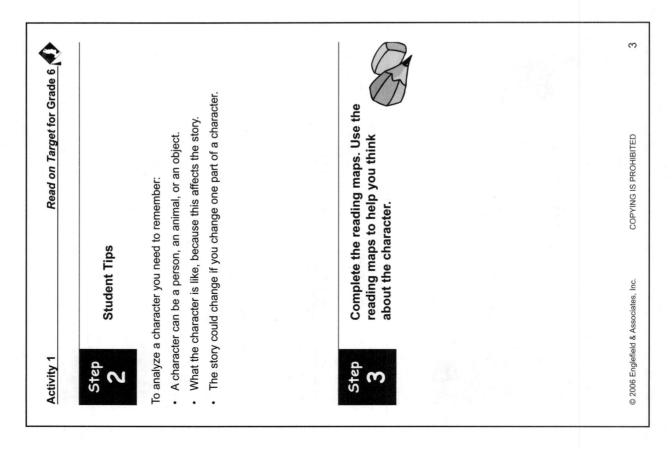

3

© 2006 Englefield & Associates, Inc.   COPYING IS PROHIBITED

Activity 1   *Read on Target* for Grade 6

Step 4

Read the following questions and write your answers.

1. What kind of person is Olivia? Give an example of something she said to support your answer.

   Olivia is kind. She made a card for her teacher. She let Ann keep her pen. She

   invited her friends to walk with her.

2. Olivia has many friends. Based on what you read about her, what kinds of things does she do to make friends?

   Olivia shares. She thinks of others and how they feel. She tries to be a good friend

   by bringing extra supplies.

3. Olivia decides to quietly place her card on her teacher's desk. What does this tell you about Olivia?

   She doesn't draw attention to her own kind deeds.

4. Olivia doesn't say anything to Ann when Ann thinks the pen is hers. What does this tell you about Olivia?

   She doesn't want to hurt Ann's feelings.

6   COPYING IS PROHIBITED   © 2006 Englefield & Associates, Inc.

Note: Student answers may vary. Example responses in italics are for use as a guide.

Activity 1   *Read on Target* for Grade 6

Map 1.2   Analyze Aspects of the Text by Examining the Characters

I read to figure out what the characters are like. I get to know them.

Think about the sentences you wrote that describe the character.

How did the character affect the story?

Olivia was kind and often did nice things for others. Because of this, most of the

story was about people getting along, sharing, and doing fun activities as a

group.

Give one quality you could change about the character.

I could change her from being a kind person to being a mean person.

How would the story change if the character had this different quality?

If Olivia were mean, she would not have made a card for her teacher, and she would

have embarrassed the other girl, Ann. Olivia may have started a fight with Ann when

Ann took Olivia's pen. Then, the story would be about fighting and conflict.

© 2006 Englefield & Associates, Inc.   COPYING IS PROHIBITED   5

Troubleshooting: Understanding Character

Teachers often become frustrated when students don't seem to understand questions about character traits of specific characters in a story. Students are often stymied by the concept of character because they have never taken the time to think about what they may already know. Tapping into prior knowledge is essential to helping students realize they do indeed have the answers inside their heads. It is worthwhile for teachers to take time ahead of the lesson to work on a mini-lesson regarding what students already sense about people's qualities.

Ask if anyone knows a person who is a really good friend. Then, write down those qualities that make this person such a good friend. Ask for examples of something he or she has done that show what a good friend is or does. Then, work the vocabulary around to translate actions into characteristic words. "My best friend never repeats anything that I tell her in confidence." What characteristic does this show? Trustworthiness, loyalty, etc.

You may have to do this a few times to develop the vocabulary of character traits, but it is worth the time invested. Once you establish a vocabulary of character traits, you can use predicting questions to see how a character might act under different circumstances. Tapping into prior knowledge helps a student to focus his or her understanding in the ways he or she will be asked to respond. You can use the student's knowledge of personal characters to explain what might cause a specific character to act the way he or she does.

Another reason students don't seem to leap into characterization is they see it as an exercise developed to torture them rather than as an integral part of story development. You can take the time to explain to students that a character's change or lack of change has a huge impact on the events that lead to the resolution of the conflict. The students still may not care, but they may understand it as a part of why they like or don't like the story. Personalizing their knowledge of a character can help to get them engaged. Tap into how they know something about a character.

Did the author describe the character? Did they understand the character through the character's thoughts or through another character's thoughts? Once students understand the story can't move forward without characters, they are generally less resistant to the concept of character.

In addition, we, as teachers, often feel if we talk about something too much, the students will use our answers rather than their own. Don't be afraid of overdoing the preparation because understanding character is varied enough and abstract enough that students can use all the practice they can get to crystallize their own ideas.

2

Analyze Aspects of the Text
by Examining Setting

Teaching Tips

What Do Students Need to Know?

Students need to understand how the setting can affect a story. To analyze aspects of the setting, students first need to name, to identify, and to describe the setting. Students need to know where and when the story takes place and that the setting can occur in the past, present, or future. Next, they need to determine the effect the setting has on the events of the story. They also need to consider how the story would be different if the setting changed. Thus, students gain a deeper understanding of the effect a setting has on the characters and events because they learn to think beyond simple identification to analysis of the setting.

Use of the Reading Map

When students analyze the setting, they look at the importance of the setting to the story. Students will need to decide how the setting influences the characters and the events that take place.

The reading map will guide the students to:

- Describe the setting.
- Tell how the setting affects the character and events.
- Tell how the characters and events would be different if the setting changed.

"You can do it!" called Jason's dad from the stands. Jason wiped the sweat from his eyes.

"I know I can do it," he thought to himself. Sure enough, on the next pitch, Jason hit the ball to the edge of the park. He ran like the wind to first base, then off to second, and finally stopping at third. "Only one more base to go, and we win the game," thought Jason. "I just know I can do it." Jason's cousin, Michael, was up to bat. He swung the bat, and the ball flew off toward right field.

"Run, Jason, run!" yelled the coach. Jason started running, dirt and dust flying everywhere. He saw the ball fly through the air. The ball was screeching toward home plate. The catcher reached for the ball but dropped it. Jason could hardly breathe as he ran toward the plate. The catcher picked up the ball just as the Jason slid home. "Safe!" yelled the umpire.

"We won!" screamed Jason's coach; players and parents ran to the field to hug each other. Suddenly, a rain cloud came out of nowhere, pouring down on the players and fans. It rained buckets and buckets. The players' dusty uniforms became coated in mud. "The only good thing about this rain," said Jason, "is that it cooled us off. I'm sure glad we didn't have to cancel the game."

The players ran out onto the field to pick up their equipment. The uniforms had become a slimy brownish-black color. The field had become a slippery, muddy mess. The players slipped and slid across the field as they picked up their equipment. "What a mess!" declared Jason.

The clouds blew away as quickly as they had come, and the rain stopped as suddenly as it had started. "Now we are all ready to eat hot dogs," cried the players. The vendors happily sold all of the food. Everyone was ready to go home.

"What a great game!" said Jason.

"I agree," said his cousin Michael. They looked at the mud on each other and laughed.

"I bet my mother will have lots of laundry to do when we get home," said Jason.

8   © 2006 Englefield & Associates, Inc.

Activity 2

Analyze Aspects of the Text by Examining Setting

I figure out how important the setting is and how the setting affects the characters and events that take place.

Step 1   Read the story "The Baseball Game."

The Baseball Game

It was a bright, sunny, summer day. Not a cloud was in the sky, and the wind was gently blowing the grass. Jason could hear the birds singing. It was a perfect day for a baseball game. Everyone in town came to watch the game. The fans sat on the bleachers wearing hats for shade. Jason was excited to be playing in the finals. He was especially glad it was not raining.

The vendors were out selling food and drinks. The hot dogs smelled good to Jason. Jason noticed they sold lots of soda pop, but people were not buying many hot dogs. Perhaps due to the heat, everyone was thirsty instead. The temperature was around 90 degrees. It was a hot day at the ballpark. The game had started at noon.

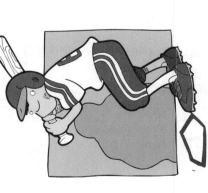

Now it was the last inning, and the score was tied. Jason stepped to the plate and waited for the first pitch. "Strike one!" shouted the umpire. Jason turned, looking at his dad and mom. He put the bat on his shoulder. Jason knew his parents had confidence in his ability to hit the ball. Jason adjusted his helmet. He was ready. Zoom! The ball whizzed by at the speed of light. Jason swung and missed as the second pitch went by. "Strike two!"

© 2006 Englefield & Associates, Inc.   7

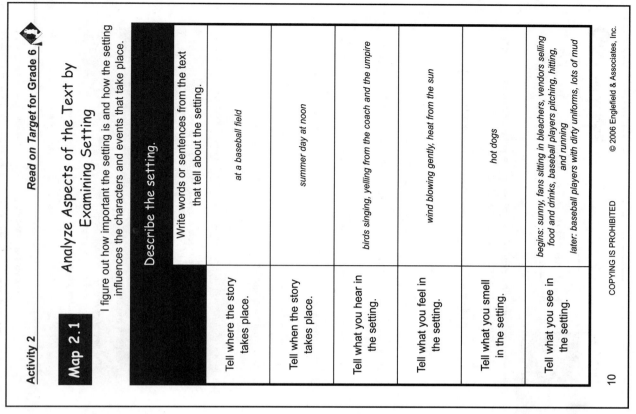

Activity 2

Map 2.1

Analyze Aspects of the Text by Examining Setting

I figure out how important the setting is and how the setting influences the characters and events that take place.

Describe the setting.

	Write words or sentences from the text that tell about the setting.
Tell where the story takes place.	*at a baseball field*
Tell when the story takes place.	*summer day at noon*
Tell what you hear in the setting.	*birds singing, yelling from the coach and the umpire*
Tell what you feel in the setting.	*wind blowing gently, heat from the sun*
Tell what you smell in the setting.	*hot dogs*
Tell what you see in the setting.	*begins: sunny, fans sitting in bleachers, vendors selling food and drinks, baseball players pitching, hitting, and running* *later: baseball players with dirty uniforms, lots of mud*

10   COPYING IS PROHIBITED   © 2006 Englefield & Associates, Inc.

Note: Student answers may vary. Example responses in italics are for use as a guide.

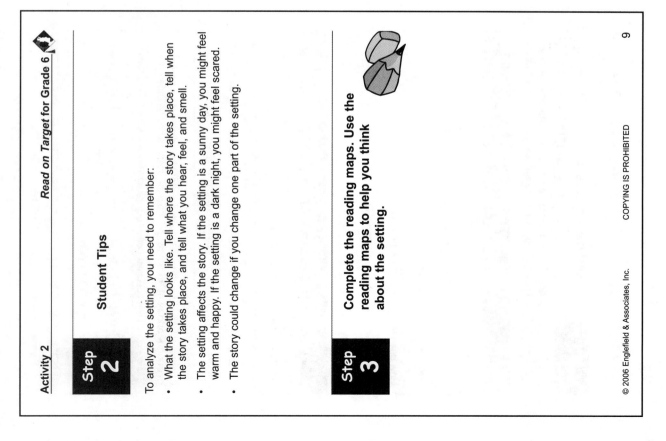

Activity 2

Step 2

Student Tips

To analyze the setting, you need to remember:

- What the setting looks like. Tell where the story takes place, tell when the story takes place, and tell what you hear, feel, and smell.
- The setting affects the story. If the setting is a sunny day, you might feel warm and happy. If the setting is a dark night, you might feel scared.
- The story could change if you change one part of the setting.

Step 3

Complete the reading maps. Use the reading maps to help you think about the setting.

© 2006 Englefield & Associates, Inc.   COPYING IS PROHIBITED   9

Activity 2   *Read on Target* **for Grade 6**

Step 4   Read the following questions and write your answers.

1. Game day was described as bright, sunny, and hot. How did the setting affect the vendor's ability to sell hot dogs?

   The vendor sold fewer hot dogs. People were thirsty, so they bought more drinks

   and fewer hot dogs.

2. How would the events in the story change if it rained at the beginning of the story?

   The game might have been cancelled. The field could be so slippery and muddy

   that someone could fall and could get hurt. More hot dogs might have been sold.

3. How would the story change if it remained a hot, sunny day throughout the story?

   The uniforms would not become muddy. The vendor would not sell many hot dogs.

   More drinks would have been sold because everyone would be hot and thirsty.

4. What aspects of the setting could be different without changing the events in the story?

   The time of day could change.

   The game could be played in a park, instead of at a baseball field.

Note: Student answers may vary. Example responses in italics are for use as a guide.

Activity 2   *Read on Target* **for Grade 6**

Map 2.2   Analyze Aspects of the Text by Examining Setting

I figure out how important the setting is and how the setting influences the characters and events that take place.

Think about the setting.

How does the setting affect the characters?

Jason is hot. He is glad it is not raining. They could finish the game. After it rains,

everyone is cooler but muddy.

How does the setting affect the events of the story?

Lots of people came to the game. Drinks were sold; hot dogs were not. The game

was finished. After it rained, all the food was sold.

Now, change the setting.

Change what the setting looks like to **a sunny day that never rains.** Tell how the story would be different.

Lots of drinks would be sold. The players uniforms would not be covered in mud after

the game. The players would be hot after the game without the rain to cool them off.

The players would not slip and slide on the field while collecting their equipment. All

the food would not be sold.

Change where the setting is (where the story takes place) to **inside a gym on Monday at 9:00 a.m.** Tell how the story would be different.

The boys might play basketball instead of baseball. People would not be as hot and

muddy. On a Monday, many people are working, so many of the people in the town

might not be able to go to the game.

Troubleshooting: Understanding the Importance of Setting

So often in popular young-adult fiction, the setting is in modern times somewhere in a modern American suburb (e.g., any scary novel out for kids today). Students don't see that setting is important to a story. However, setting, the time and place of action in a story, may or may not be important to a story's development, mood, or atmosphere. The details of setting may contribute to the conflict (as with *Gone with the Wind*, for example) and can clue the reader into a character's motivation, and even influence a character's thoughts. It is important for students to see that a story may be so universal it could have happened anywhere; or, setting can be so integral to the plot, a story could only have happened during that time and place.

Again, tapping into the student's prior knowledge can help a student understand the importance of setting. Often, just a little preparatory conversation can take students right where you want to be: accessing their own banks of knowledge to draw out ideas about something new.

Ask students if they have ever experienced something frightening in the darkness of night, but when the morning came, things seemed completely different. Be sure to let them take this away in their imaginations. Another question to get them engaged is to ask them about places they have been that felt wrong and unhappy, or warm and cozy. Ask them to think about how those places affected their moods, feelings, and actions.

3

Analyze Aspects of the Text by Examining the Plot

Teaching Tips

What Do Students Need to Know?

Students need to know plot is the **chain of events** that happen in the story. Sometimes, the events are in **chronological order**. Other times, an event from the past can occur first, such as with the **flashback technique**. The author may also mix up the order of the events. Students will need to consider the sequence of events and the effect the events have on the story. Teaching certain key words, which indicate the sequence of events, will help students keep track of the chain of events. Have students look for key words such as **first**, **second**, **next**, **then**, **before**, **while**, **later**, and **last** to keep track of the order in which the events occurred. Students may consider how the story would change if the events were in a different order or even left out of the story. Students may also consider what would happen if the characters' actions were different.

Use of the Reading Map

When students analyze the plot, they describe the chain of events and consider how these events affect the story. The order of the events and the character's actions are important elements for understanding the story.

The reading map will guide students to:

- Write the chain of events in the boxes in the correct sequence as presented in the story. As the number of events increases or decreases, the number of boxes may need to be increased or decreased.

- Choose an event to happen earlier or later.

- Tell how the story would be different if one of the events happened earlier or later.

- Take an event out of the story.

- Tell how the story is different when one of the events is left out of the story.

- Tell what would happen if the character's actions were different.

Activity 3

At last, we reached the top. "Oh," said my cousins, "the view is incredible!" We could see the town far below. Our aunt and uncle's bright yellow house and big red barn stood out against the green hills below. We could also see small rivers and a lake. The farmland down below looked like a green patchwork quilt. It was exciting for us to discover all the beautiful things to see when hiking. We lingered there enjoying all the beauty.

As we started down the mountain, my cousins and I realized the sun was sinking lower, and we were lost! We no longer could see the town or our aunt and uncle's house. The trees seemed to close up around us. We were scared! All I could think about was getting home. "Oh no!" I said. My only thought was my fear of not being able to descend the mountain before the weather turned to snow. If snow came, the footholds on the trail would be as slippery as glass. "Let's get going!" I cried. I had no idea where I was going. Suddenly, I remembered that I brought the compass. "Hooray!" I cried, "I think we are going to find our way home."

Finally, we made it home to the farm. A chilly breeze had started to blow, pelting sharp rain on us, and we could see snow swirling at the top of the mountain. We were glad to be inside in a warm house. Our aunt and uncle were glad that we packed hiking supplies, especially the compass. Those supplies helped make the hike a success. What an adventure! But I was relieved to be home safe and sound.

Activity 3

Analyze Aspects of the Text by Examining Plot
I read to figure out the chain of events; what will happen next.

Step 1   Read the story "A Hike in the Woods."

A Hike in the Woods

I can still remember the day we went hiking in the woods. It was in the late autumn. The sun was a bright lemon yellow, and the sky was as blue as the ocean. It was a good day to be outside. My cousins, Samantha, Joey, Michael, and Hannah, and I were visiting our aunt and uncle. They live on a farm near the wooded mountains. We decided it would be a great idea to hike up to the very top of the mountain closest to their farm.

First, we had to gather our hiking gear. We would need hiking shoes, warm hats, food, water, and most importantly, a compass. It took most of the morning to find everything we needed, but eventually we found everything we thought was important for our hike. I could not believe how much hiking gear we needed!

Next, we said goodbye to our aunt and uncle as we went off to hike up the mountain. The ground around the farm was covered with a blanket of yellow asters. The gentle breeze made them move as if they were dancing in the fields. Bluebirds and robins poked their sharp beaks into the ground searching for worms. The cows chewed lazily on the tall grass as we passed by.

As we continued up the mountain, we noticed the trees were taller and grew closer together than they had at the altitude of the farm. It was just like looking at a wall of wood. I thought it would be a great place to have a tree house. As we climbed higher and higher, it became colder and colder. I even saw snow on the ground. It was time to stop, to eat, and to rest. We decided to put on our hats. I certainly was glad we packed them. We then ate our food, which consisted of sandwiches, chips, cookies, and drinks. It tasted delicious, and we ate every bite. After eating and resting, we continued our trip. It was a perfect place to hike.

COPYING IS PROHIBITED   **25**

Map 3.1

Analyze Aspects of the Text by Examining Plot
I read to figure out the chain of events; what will happen next.

Activity 3

First Event

The cousins decide to go on a hike.

Next Event

The cousins gather up their hiking gear, shoes, warm hats, food, and compass.

Next Event

The cousins rest. They eat, put on their hats, and continue to climb to the top.

Next Event

When they start down the mountain, the cousins are lost.

Next Event

The compass is used to figure out which direction to go.

Last Event

The cousins return home just as it begins to snow.

16

Note: Student answers may vary. Example responses in italics are for use as a guide.

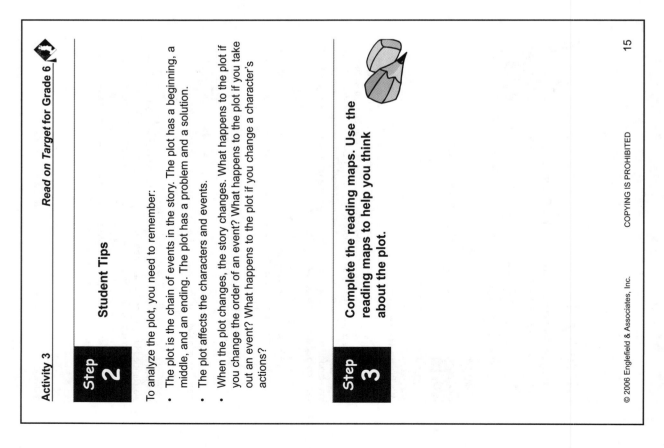

Activity 3

Step 2

Student Tips

To analyze the plot, you need to remember:

- The plot is the chain of events in the story. The plot has a beginning, a middle, and an ending. The plot has a problem and a solution.

- The plot affects the characters and events.

- When the plot changes, the story changes. What happens to the plot if you change the order of an event? What happens to the plot if you take out an event? What happens to the plot if you change a character's actions?

Step 3

Complete the reading maps. Use the reading maps to help you think about the plot.

15

Activity 3   *Read on Target* **for Grade 6**

Step 4

Read the following questions and write your answers.

1. Why did the cousins pack hiking gear prior to starting out on their hike?

   They wanted to take everything that was important for the hike.

2. What could have happened if the cousins had forgotten to pack food?

   If they were hungry, when they became lost, they might not have had enough energy to continue. The story would be about how the cousins looked for food on the trail.

3. How do the cousins find their way home?

   They use a compass to help them find the correct direction home.

4. How would the story be different if a sudden snowstorm occurred while the cousins were at the top of the mountain?

   The story would have included more events related to the snowstorm. For example, the characters may get lost or cold and may need to survive in the snow. They may need to find warm shelter.

18   COPYING IS PROHIBITED   © 2006 Englefield & Associates, Inc.

Note: Student answers may vary. Example responses in italics are for use as a guide.

Activity 3   *Read on Target* **for Grade 6**

Map 3.2

Analyze Aspects of the Text by Examining Plot

I read to figure out the chain of events; what will happen next.

Change the Plot.

Choose an event to happen earlier or later. Write the event you choose.

later: eating food, resting, putting on hats

How might the story be different if one of the events happened earlier or later?

If these events happened later, the cousins might get cold, hungry, and tired. Instead of the story being about getting lost, it could be about how the cousins tried to stay warm or tried to find food.

Take an event out of the story. Write the event you choose.

The hiking gear is not packed.

How might the story be different if one of the events is left out of the story?

The cousins cannot find their way home without the compass. Now the story is about cousins being lost in the woods for a longer period of time. Maybe a search party is formed to find them.

What would happen if the characters' actions were different?

If the cousins did not take the time to eat and drink, they may become dehydrated or sick.

© 2006 Englefield & Associates, Inc.   COPYING IS PROHIBITED   17

Troubleshooting: Understanding the Plot

Understanding plot is usually not difficult for students. They see it as the "what happened" in the story. Most story plots follow a traditional pattern. Students who understand the events often draw a blank when looking at them analytically. They don't think in terms of plot progression. The beginning, often referred to as "exposition," sets the stage, introduces characters and setting, and introduces the readers to the problem. Sometimes, an author starts slowly to let the reader know all that is necessary to understand the plot development. This is the point at which students say they are bored and don't like the story. The "rising action" is where the events build suspense and the plot "thickens." The "climax" is the turning point, the point at which the action reaches a peak or there is a change in the direction of the action. Then, the falling action leads to the "resolution" ("denouement"), which ties up all the loose ends and solves the problem. If you can help students understand the significance of some of the elements of plot, you can help them get to higher-level concepts such as underlying theme or even author's attitude.

The biggest problem most teachers encounter with inexperienced students in understanding the plot is they tend to want to provide too much information. Very often, they want to give a blow-by-blow account of what happened in the story. Encourage them to give only major events that lead to the solving of the problem (conflict). You can show them the difference by using Sergeant Friday's idea of, "Just the facts, ma'am." Ask them to tell about their morning and getting to school. Most kids will say something like, "I got up a little late, got dressed, grabbed a pastry, and ran out to catch the bus." You can ask them to embellish with details that are unnecessary, such as, "The alarm rang at 6:30, and I was so sleepy I pushed the snooze two times." They begin to see plot events as "the facts" that lead to the solving of the problem.

State test questions are generally focused on a manipulation of the plot incidents to see if students understand the significance of major events, such as how they influence future actions and how they are resolved.

You can help your students on a daily basis by asking them how any narrative situation would be different if a critical person wasn't there or if a significant event had happened differently or not at all. Drawing on students' personal experiences can help noticeably in improving responses to a written story.

Analyze Aspects of the Text by Examining the Problem/Solution

Teaching Tips

What Do Students Need to Know?

Students will need to understand that the problem (conflict) can be a situation the character wants to change or something the character wants to do. The solution can be an action or decision that helps the character understand how the problem is solved. Understanding the character's problems and how the problems are solved will help students follow the plot. In fiction and poetry, characters may face problems that need solutions. The primary problem is usually established early in the story. As the story progresses, additional problems related to the main problem may occur. The solution will occur when there is an action or decision that makes it clear how the problem can be resolved.

Use of the Reading Maps

When students analyze the problem and solution, they first describe the problem. Next, they need to see how the events help solve the problem. Then, they determine what action is taken to bring about a solution and they describe the solution. Finally, students will be guided to determine what effect solving the problem in a different way has on changing the events and solution.

The reading map will guide students to:

- Read the definition of the problem and the solution at the top of the reading map.
- Write the problem of the story.
- Write the events that helped solve the problem.
- Write the solution of the story.
- Change the problem by making up a different problem.
- Write a made-up problem.
- Write how the events would be different if the problem changed.
- Write how the solution would be different if the problem changed.

Activity 4

Analyze Aspects of the Text by Examining Problem/Solution

I read to figure out the problem and how it is solved.

Step 1 Read the story "One School Morning."

One School Morning

It was a gloomy, gusty, gray, and rainy morning. The wind whipped around the trees and sounded like a train whistle. It was the kind of day for sleeping late, and Pam's warm covers offered her a cozy nest to stay in all day long.

Unfortunately, it was a school day, and Pam was sound asleep in her bed. The alarm clock sat silently on the night stand beside her bed. The noise of the wind woke Pam. "Oh no!" said Pam as she rubbed the sleep from her eyes. "I am going to be late to school!" She checked her alarm clock to find out why it had not done its job. She knew she had set it the night before. As she pressed the button to see the time the alarm was set for, she discovered she was right—she had set her alarm the night before . . . for 7:15 p.m.! She ran to the window just in time to see the back of the school bus as it pulled away from her house.

Pam rushed around the house. She needed to find her clothes and school supplies. She thought to herself, "I should have laid out these clothes last night. What am I going to do?" Her sock drawer was a mess, but she finally managed to find two matching socks. She saw one shoe under her bed, but it took her a few moments to find its

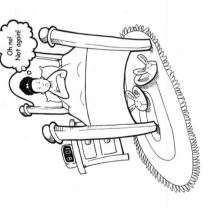

match, which had somehow ended up downstairs behind the couch. "Why me?" Pam moaned. "Of all mornings, why does everything have to be so difficult this morning!"

"Now, I am almost ready to go. All I need to do is make my lunch," said Pam. No time for anything fancy this morning. She quickly grabbed the jars of peanut butter and jelly from the refrigerator. Her fingers flew as she spread first peanut butter and then jelly on two pieces of white bread. She returned the jars to the fridge and was going to rinse off the knife when it suddenly slipped from her hand, smearing grape jelly down the front of her favorite T-shirt. "No time to worry about it now," Pam thought to herself as she continued to pack her lunch. An apple, a small bag of chips, and a juice box made her lunch complete. She grabbed her backpack and ran out the door with her lunch in hand.

As she ran off the front porch, she tripped on a branch that had fallen to the ground during the storm the night before. She fell right into a fresh puddle of mud. To make matters worse, she had landed on her lunch. The bag began to turn a strange purple color. She peeked inside to discover not only had she smashed her sandwich, but her juice box had exploded, and the jelly and juice were combining to form a sickening purple soup. What a mess! Pam had no choice but to go back in the house and start all over again! Now, she was really late.

As she entered the school building, the principal asked, "Why are you late?" Pam wished she had not overslept. "This is the fourth time this school year that you have been late," said the principal.

"I know," said Pam. She continued, "I just woke up late again."

"I want you to think how you can solve this problem," said the principal. Pam agreed to think about her problem.

As she went to class, she thought about several ways to solve her problem. One way could be to ask her parents to call and excuse her. Another way could be to sneak into school. She did not think these would be good solutions. Pam asked her friends what they would do. Her friends said they could stop by her house in the morning to make sure she was awake. They thought she might want to ask her parents to help her too. Most importantly, they said it was up to Pam to make sure she set her clock correctly!

When Pam got home from school that day, she decided to have a fresh start. She threw out her old alarm clock, which had been giving her problems, and asked her parents to buy her a new one. Each night, she carefully set the alarm to wake her up on time. Her family and friends also helped to make sure she was getting up on time. Sure enough, the new plan worked, and she was never late to school again.

Activity 4   *Read on Target* for Grade 6

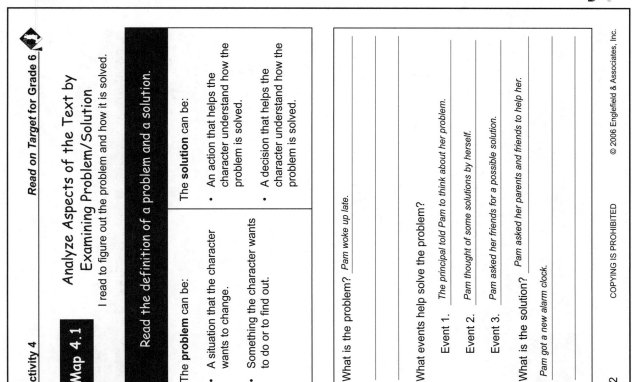

Activity 4 *Read on Target for Grade 6*

Map 4.1

Analyze Aspects of the Text by Examining Problem/Solution

I read to figure out the problem and how it is solved.

Read the definition of a problem and a solution.

The **problem** can be:

- A situation that the character wants to change.
- Something the character wants to do or to find out.

The **solution** can be:

- An action that helps the character understand how the problem is solved.
- A decision that helps the character understand how the problem is solved.

What is the problem? *Pam woke up late.*

What events help solve the problem?

Event 1. *The principal told Pam to think about her problem.*

Event 2. *Pam thought of some solutions by herself.*

Event 3. *Pam asked her friends for a possible solution.*

What is the solution? *Pam asked her parents and friends to help her.*

Pam got a new alarm clock.

22 COPYING IS PROHIBITED © 2006 Englefield & Associates, Inc.

Note: Student answers may vary. Example responses in italics are for use as a guide.

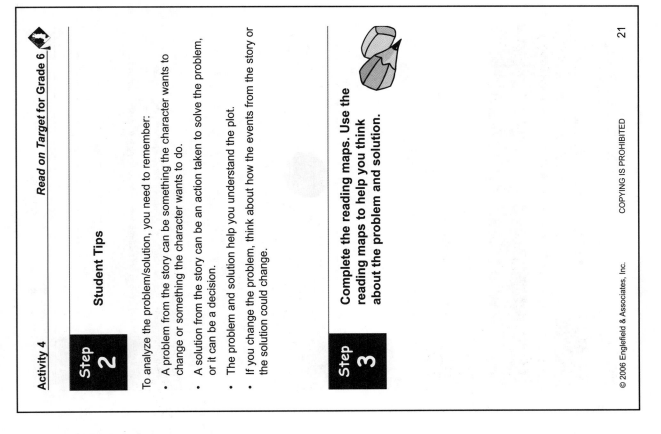

Activity 4 *Read on Target for Grade 6*

Step 2

Student Tips

To analyze the problem/solution, you need to remember:

- A problem from the story can be something the character wants to change or something the character wants to do.
- A solution from the story can be an action taken to solve the problem, or it can be a decision.
- The problem and solution help you understand the plot.
- If you change the problem, think about how the events from the story or the solution could change.

Step 3

Complete the reading maps. Use the reading maps to help you think about the problem and solution.

© 2006 Englefield & Associates, Inc. COPYING IS PROHIBITED 21

Activity 4 — *Read on Target* for Grade 6

Step 4 — **Read the following questions and write your answers.**

1. What is Pam's problem?

   She did not get up on time.

2. Pam thought about several solutions as a way to solve her problem. List the solutions that she considered.

   She could have asked her parents to call the school and excuse her for the day.

   She could sneak into school.

3. What did Pam's friends suggest as a way to solve Pam's problem?

   They could stop by her house in the morning.

4. If the problem changed to become Pam forgetting her homework, how would the events be different?

   Pam might get a bad grade. Pam might be given a detention or have to skip recess

   in order to complete her homework.

24 — COPYING IS PROHIBITED — © 2006 Englefield & Associates, Inc.

Note: Student answers may vary. Example responses in italics are for use as a guide.

Activity 4 — *Read on Target* for Grade 6

Map 4.2

Analyze Aspects of the Text by Examining Problem/Solution

I read to figure out the problem and how it is solved.

Change the problem by making up a different problem.

Write your made-up problem on these lines.

Pam did not get her homework finished.

How would the events be different?

Event 1. *When Pam woke up, she realized she had not done her homework the night before.*

Event 2. *She went to school with blank papers.*

Event 3. *Pam was given a detention because she did not have her homework to turn in.*

How would the solution be different?

Pam wouldn't ask for a clock. She would ask for an assignment pad or a calendar to write down her assignments. She would try to remember to do her homework.

© 2006 Englefield & Associates, Inc. — COPYING IS PROHIBITED — 23

Troubleshooting: Understanding Problem/Solution

Teachers trying to help students understand problem and solution most often comment that students don't seem to get the big picture. This is usually related to the fact that they didn't really understand the plot, and they identify an insignificant part of the plot as the solution. If students read a story about rushing to school and you ask what the problem of that narrative was, most would tell you it is that the character was almost late to school. However, the problem really was that the student got up late. If the students were going to continue the story and solve the problem, it would include some kind of compensating action to overcome the late start. That could be getting a new alarm clock, finding a tricky way to sneak into school, or asking a parent to call in an excuse. Students will benefit by teachers focusing on the correct problem prior to continuing with the solution.

Again, draw on the experience of the students. Ask the students, "If one of the plot elements was different, how would that affect the solution to the story?" Using the problem of the story, you might draw upon their predicting skills of how this problem could be solved.

Analyze Aspects of the Text by Examining the Point of View

Teaching Tips

What Do Students Need to Know?

Point of view is the writer's choice of speaker in the story. It is the angle (viewpoint) from which the story is told. Who is telling the story can affect what the student finds out about the character and the events. Teaching the key words that indicate the author's choice of speaker will help students determine the point of view. By figuring out the point of view, students will gain an understanding of how much the author wishes to reveal about the character and events. Students need to determine the author's point of view. They will then be able to determine if the author caused suspense by providing the reader with information that some characters do not have (third person) or if the author allowed the reader to step into the shoes of the character and see the events and actions that the character sees (first person). Students need to be able to determine why the author wrote from this point of view and how changing the point of view affects the story.

Use of the Reading Maps

When students analyze the point of view, they need to determine who is telling the story and how much is revealed about each character and the events. Students will be guided to understand why the author wrote from the point of view and how a different point of view would affect the story.

The reading map will guide students to:

- Read the definitions and key word pronouns of each point of view.

- Circle the point of view in the story.

- Write one or more sentences from the story that helped them figure out the author's point of view. Have students review the definition of a point of view and find key pronouns to give them clues for determining the point of view.

- Tell why the author writes from the point of view.

- Tell how changing the point of view would affect the story.

The boys continued to wander through the intricate maze of passages. They were having little luck in their search. Just then, Carlos noticed a small opening near the floor of the passage they were in. The boys were hesitant to crawl through the narrow opening, but they were not about to give up. On hands and knees, they crawled through the ever-narrowing passageway. They continued on for what seemed like hundreds of yards. Finally, the passage opened up into a large, cavernous room. The three boys emerged and shined their flashlights around the room. On the walls, they saw primitive drawings and designs of people and animals. They stood in awe as they gazed at the ancient gallery.

Suddenly, they heard a loud clap of thunder. Peter looked up with a troubled frown. "I think we better look at the weather. These drawings will be here later." Carlos was wondering how in the world they would find their way out of the cave.

Peter was beginning to get scared. He was wishing he had not suggested to his friends that they search for the cave. Jacob thought, "The string will surely save the day. I know just how to get out of here." Jacob noticed that his friends were quiet. He said, "What's wrong?"

His friends replied, "We are lost in this cave!" They just wanted to go home before the storm got any worse.

Jacob grinned at them and pulled out the string. "This is tied to a tree at the front of the cave. All we need to do is just follow the string."

Carlos whooped, "You saved the day!" Jacob was right. The boys followed the trail of string out of the cave. They made it home before the rain started. All the boys were glad Jacob remembered to use the string. He had indeed saved the day!

26

Activity 5

Analyze Aspects of the Text by Examining Point of View

I figure out the author's choice of speaker. I also think why the author chose to write from this point of view and how the story would be different if the story were told from another point of view.

Step 1   Read the story "The Cave."

The Cave

Jacob and his friends, Carlos and Peter, had a great interest in studying plants, rocks, and small animals that lived in the nearby mountains. They were also very interested in the terrain and history of the surrounding area. Jacob became very excited one day after reading about paintings found in a nearby cave. "Look at the article in this newspaper. There are paintings that must have been done by early mankind," said Peter, showing the article to his friends.

Carlos replied, "I think the paintings are called hieroglyphics."

"Let's see if we can find the cave," said Peter. Carlos was just a little afraid he might get lost. He did not want his friends to know how he felt because he did not want to be teased. Jacob was a little anxious and would rather have stayed behind. He didn't want to be made fun of either. As a result, he agreed to go in search of the cave.

"Let's go!" they cried. The boys began searching for the cave. Just then, at the foot of a bluff, they saw the cave.

"Here it is!" shouted Peter. The boys scrambled up to the cave.

Jacob thought to himself, "We had better make sure we don't lose our way. I have a string in my pocket that we can use to find our way back in case we get lost in the cave."

Entering the dark gloomy cave, they could see several passages with long dark walkways. "If we find more of the drawings, we will be famous," said Jacob.

"No kidding?" questioned Peter. "Well," he thought, "if I am going to be famous, then I better keep moving in this cave." "Come along," he said aloud, "let's keep going."

25

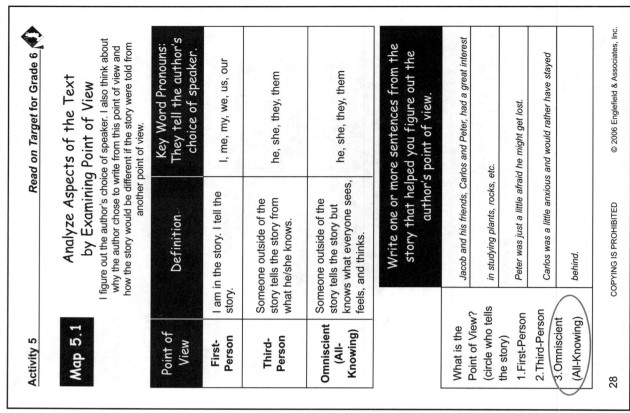

Activity 5   *Read on Target* for Grade 6

Analyze Aspects of the Text by Examining Point of View

I figure out the author's choice of speaker. I also think about why the author chose to write from this point of view and how the story would be different if the story were told from another point of view.

Map 5.1

Point of View	Definition	Key Word Pronouns: They tell the author's choice of speaker.
First-Person	I am in the story. I tell the story.	I, me, my, we, us, our
Third-Person	Someone outside of the story tells the story from what he/she knows.	he, she, they, them
Omniscient (All-Knowing)	Someone outside of the story tells the story but knows what everyone sees, feels, and thinks.	he, she, they, them

Write one or more sentences from the story that helped you figure out the author's point of view.

What is the Point of View? (circle who tells the story) 1. First-Person 2. Third-Person 3. Omniscient (All-Knowing)	*Jacob and his friends, Carlos and Peter, had a great interest* *in studying plants, rocks, etc.* *Peter was just a little afraid he might get lost.* *Carlos was a little anxious and would rather have stayed* *behind.*

28

Note: Student answers may vary. Example responses in italics are for use as a guide.

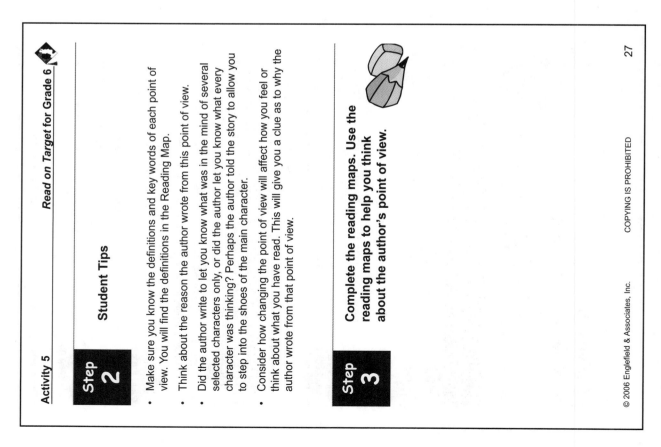

Activity 5   *Read on Target* for Grade 6

Step 2 | **Student Tips**

- Make sure you know the definitions and key words of each point of view. You will find the definitions in the Reading Map.
- Think about the reason the author wrote from this point of view.
- Did the author write to let you know what was in the mind of several selected characters only, or did the author let you know what every character was thinking? Perhaps the author told the story to allow you to step into the shoes of the main character.
- Consider how changing the point of view will affect how you feel or think about what you have read. This will give you a clue as to why the author wrote from that point of view.

Step 3 | **Complete the reading maps. Use the reading maps to help you think about the author's point of view.**

27

Read on Target **for Grade 6**

Activity 5

Step 4

Read the following questions and write your answers.

1. How did you figure out the point of view of this story?

I checked to see if the author described all the characters' thoughts and feelings. I

looked for pronouns such as he, she, and they.

2. At first, only Jacob knew he had used a string to help him find the way out of the cave. How did you feel knowing that Carlos and Peter were worried about becoming lost in the cave?

I felt the tension and was worried for the boys because they did not know Jacob

could help them.

3. How might the story be different if both Carlos and Jacob knew that Peter was afraid he might get lost going to the cave?

They might have told him they were scared, too. Then, the boys might have stayed

home.

4. What point of view would an author most likely use if he or she wrote this story as an autobiography?

The author would probably use first person to write the story as an autobiography.

30   COPYING IS PROHIBITED   © 2006 Englefield & Associates, Inc.

Note: Student answers may vary. Example responses in italics are for use as a guide.

Read on Target **for Grade 6**

Activity 5

Map 5.2

Analyze Aspects of the Text by Examining Point of View

I figure out the author's choice of speaker. I also think about why the author chose to write from this point of view and how the story would be different if the story were told from another point of view.

Why did the author write from this point of view?

So the person reading the story will know how all the characters feel, think, and see.

Change the point of view to first-person. How is the story different?

If the story was told in first person, the reader would have a slanted perspective.

If the story was told in third person, the reader would only understand one

character's perspective.

© 2006 Englefield & Associates, Inc.   COPYING IS PROHIBITED   29

Troubleshooting: Analyzing Point of View

Students can usually determine the author's point of view if given a short review. However, analyzing the reason an author writes from one point of view or another, or how changing the point of view would affect the story, requires serious thought that discourages many students. The solution is to engage your students in simple examples that will help them see possibilities for using one point of view over another. For example, tell a two-minute, chilling, first-person ghost story such as sensing a strange electrical kind of stimulation, then going upstairs and feeling a shocking temperature drop, then seeing an eerie blue light that seemed to be a transparent form of half of a person. Your students will most likely ask you, "Really? You saw a real ghost?" Using the first person makes an unlikely story seem real. People have a tendency to be trusting of the written word, especially when it seems to be an eyewitness account. Edgar Allan Poe used this technique masterfully to engage his readers in the twists of the human mind. Using this little technique will show your students that using "I" (first person) makes a fantasy seem more believable, such as, "I know this is true because I was there." Another reason an author may use first person is to make the narrative more personable by sharing personal thoughts and feelings. Memoirs would fall into this category; so would autobiographies.

Third person (when limited) allows the reader to know what is in the minds of selected characters only. The reader is viewing the events from a step back. A writer may write about only what is observable or write what is in the mind of only one character and report on observations of other characters. This way, a writer can build suspense in a story or remain somewhat aloof or out of the action and therefore be a voice of reason amidst chaos. Try having the students write a simple paragraph using first-person pronouns (I, me, my). Then, ask them to step back and substitute third-person pronouns for all the first-person pronouns. Ask them to comment on what they see as the differences. Does it make the paragraph better or worse? Why? Does it change the feeling of the paragraph at all? Biographies and many narratives use third person.

Third person omniscient (all-knowing) allows the reader to know everything that all characters are thinking or doing. The reader and the author know everything that is happening in all the characters' minds, but the other characters do not. Ask students if they have ever watched a movie where a character is going to do something or is going somewhere where the audience knows he or she shouldn't, but the character doesn't know. What sort of feelings does this type of approach bring to the viewer? Authors use this technique for many reasons, but giving the reader a sense of being more knowledgeable than the characters is an effect of omniscient point of view. Suspense can be built in this way, too.

The most effective approach to helping students understand the effects of point of view is to use simple examples and extend them to the pieces of literature students are reading. Be prepared to guide and nudge your students, because this is not an easy thing for children to do. They often don't even notice what point of view an author uses.

6 Analyze Aspects of the Text by Examining the Theme

Teaching Tips

What Do Students Need to Know?

The **theme** is the overall message or major point of the story. It tells the primary message of the story and holds it together. The theme can be stated in a single phrase or a sentence. The theme may be implied or stated directly in the text. Students can figure out the theme by looking at the lessons the character learned or the lesson the student learned. Remind students to look at the title as a clue to figuring out the theme of the story.

Use of the Reading Map

When students analyze the theme, they identify the overall message that the author is trying to communicate. Students will need to consider the lesson the author is portraying.

The reading map will guide students to:

- Name some of the ideas from the text that tell what the story is about.

- Write the lesson the character or characters learned.

- Write a sentence telling what the message of the story or theme is about.

Activity 6 | *Read on Target* for Grade 6

Suddenly, Buster jumped right out of the tree. That squirrel landed right on the back of the black and white ten-pound rabbit. Unbelievably, Thumper had a squirrel right on his back! It looked like a cowboy riding a bronco horse in a rodeo. Buster's little squirrel legs held on tight. That angry squirrel fussed with Thumper, while all the time Thumper was bucking, hopping, and running all around the yard. Everyone laughed. It was the funniest sight we had ever seen.

Soon enough, Thumper stopped bucking and Buster jumped off. The rodeo ride was over! Thumper quickly hopped away from Buster's food bowl, all the while seeming confused about what had just happened. From that day on, Thumper never ate Buster's food, and Buster has never ridden on top of Thumper again. It looks like Thumper has learned his lesson.

32　　COPYING IS PROHIBITED　　© 2006 Englefield & Associates, Inc.

Activity 6

Analyze Aspects of the Text by Examining Theme

I figure out the overall message the author is telling me.

Step 1 Read the story "The Rodeo Ride."

The Rodeo Ride

In my backyard, you can see a lot of animals running around, the funniest of which are a squirrel and a rabbit. I call the squirrel Buster and consider him to be a part of the family, and our family rabbit is named Thumper.

Usually, Buster the squirrel scampers along the leafy branches of the trees. He peers out from his holes in the back of the lawn. Then, he jumps from tree to tree, collecting nuts and berries. Buster is a very busy squirrel.

Our rabbit, Thumper, is black and white. He weighs about 10 pounds. Thumper is soft, furry, and hops around the yard very fast. He nibbles on grass and plants in the yard and runs out of sight when he senses danger.

Our backyard can be full of fun and adventure for the animals. Sometimes, Thumper the rabbit likes to take Buster's food. Because Thumper can hop very fast, Buster has trouble catching him. This seems to make Buster mad enough that he sometimes sits on a tree limb, chattering angrily at Thumper from a distance.

Just yesterday, Mr. Nathan put out the sunflower seeds and nuts for Buster to eat. He put the food bowl under a crabapple tree. Thumper was quietly watching the food bowl. He decided to investigate the food bowl, but he did not see Buster in the tree above, so he hopped right up to the food bowl. Buster looked down at Thumper. He seemed so angry that this time, he didn't even chatter at Thumper. I'll bet Buster was thinking about how to teach Thumper a lesson for stealing his food. Buster appeared angrier every minute because Thumper continued to eat the food. He was going to finish all of it if nothing stopped him. Buster began to chatter angrily. Thumper didn't seem to listen, he just nibbled away at the food in the bowl.

© 2006 Englefield & Associates, Inc.　　COPYING IS PROHIBITED　　31

Activity 6

Map 6

Analyze Aspects of the Text by Examining Theme

I figure out the overall message that the author is telling me.

Name some of the ideas that you learned from the story.

The title is "The Rodeo Ride."

Buster was getting angrier every minute because Thumper

was going to eat all of Buster's food.

He began to chatter angrily. Thumper should have listened,

but he just nibbled away at the food in the bowl.

What lessons did the character or characters learn?

Thumper was quietly watching the food bowl; Thumper never ate Buster's

food, and Buster never again rode on top of Thumper; Thumper quickly

hopped away from Buster's food bowl.

Write a sentence telling what you think the theme of the story is.

Don't take something that is not yours.

34

COPYING IS PROHIBITED   © 2006 Englefield & Associates, Inc.

Note: Student answers may vary. Example responses in italics are for use as a guide.

Activity 6

Step 2

Student Tips

To analyze theme, you need to remember:

- There are important ideas from the story. Look for words that tell about the story. Look for repeated words.

- The character might learn lessons. Think about how the character feels and thinks. Think about what happened to the character.

- There is an overall message of the story.

Step 3

Complete the reading map. Use the reading map to help you think about the theme.

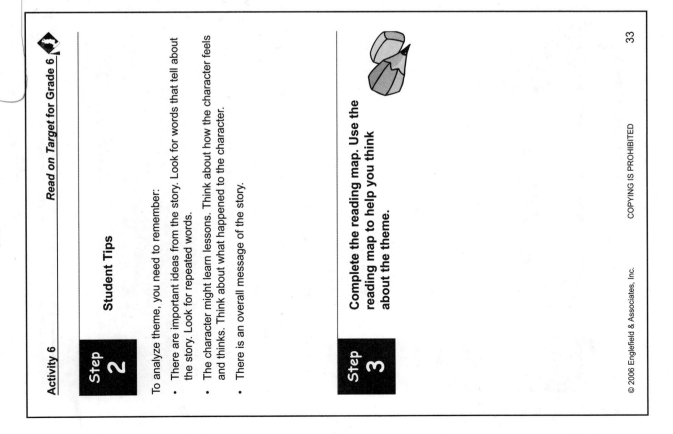

33

© 2006 Englefield & Associates, Inc.   COPYING IS PROHIBITED

Note: Student answers may vary. Example responses in italics are for use as a guide.

Activity 6

Step 4

Read the following questions and write your answers.

1. What did Thumper do with Buster's food?

    Thumper ate Buster's food.

2. How did Buster react to Thumper eating his food?

    Buster was angry because the food was his and if Thumper ate all of the food,

    Buster would not have food to eat.

3. What lesson did Thumper learn?

    Thumper never ate Buster's food, and Buster never again rode on top of Thumper.

    Thumper quickly hopped away from Buster's food bowl, all the while wondering

    what had just happened. (Students are expected to choose one of these answers.)

4. What is the theme of the story?

    Don't take something that is not yours.

35

Troubleshooting: Understanding the Theme

Since reading and interpreting are subjective, be prepared to have an open mind when you ask your students what the theme of a piece of writing is. Students need to ask themselves what message the literary piece is trying to get across. The theme may be very clearly stated or it may never be stated, only implied, which leads readers to interpret the message in different ways.

There are some helpful suggestions you can make to your students. When students draw a blank on what the theme of the story is, have them skim the story for phrases and sentences that say something about life or people in general. Look for repeated words or phrases that emphasize important ideas or feelings. Think back to the events that happen to the main character and what lessons he or she may have learned. Using this input can help a student sort out what the author was trying to get across.

Another approach is to have your students think about what they read. Encourage them to use one sentence to sum up what the author is trying to say in the story. Students should understand that themes tend to be more universal, applying in a larger sense than any specific incident in a plot.

You might even liken theme to the moral of the story in an Aesop's fable, such as "The Grasshopper and the Ant." The message is clear that even though the ants took pity on the grasshopper, their industriousness is rewarded by having enough on hand for the hard times, while the grasshopper's laziness could have cost him his life. You could even draw on a student's experience by asking a student what lesson he or she learned from an event. At any rate, any supported case for a theme should be taken seriously, even if you personally had other ideas. This helps students to realize their ideas, when supported logically, have value.

Teaching Tips

What Do Students Need to Know?

Students become engaged in the story by making inferences. Students connect information in the story to their experiences and knowledge. Inferring involves students **reading** about the **clues** in the story and using **experiences** or **knowledge** to make a **guess** about **what is happening** in the story. Real-life experiences help students develop a broader depth of knowledge. Oftentimes, students do not have opportunities to experience or to gain knowledge of the information in a text that is used in conjunction with an inference question. To assist students in developing an extensive base of information, teachers may need to provide real-life experiences, discussion, or pictures correlating with the information in the story. For example, before reading a story, teachers may need to present materials or pictures about the information. Students need to be questioned about their experiences during the guided instruction phase of completing the inferring map. To increase an understanding of the clues, teachers need to point to the book's cover and title and ask students what they think the story is about. In addition, teachers can identify a clue from the book and ask why it is a clue, or how the clue helped students make a guess about what is happening in the story. This focuses students on the demands of clues, experiences, and knowledge.

Use of the Reading Maps

When students infer, they often use clues and experiences or knowledge in the beginning of the story. As students continue to read, they find additional clues and draw upon their prior experiences or knowledge. Then, they can include or exclude their guesses about what is happening in the story.

The reading map will guide students to:

- Read a sentence or paragraph to find a clue about the meaning of the story.

- Write the clue in the clue box.

- Write about an experience or knowledge the student has of a similar thing.

- Put together the clue and experience or knowledge to make an inference.

- Read more of the paragraph to see if the inference is correct.

Activity 7a

Infer from the Text

I read clues and use what I know to figure out what is happening in the story.

Step 1 Read the story "The Best Day."

The Best Day

It was cold, and the yard was covered in white. The ground looked as smooth as frosting with its tiny swirls and peaks. It was so deep that people were having difficulty walking outside. Seth peeked out from his blanket. The warmth was in sharp contrast to the frost that edged the windows, leaving only a limited view of the outside world. Marcus looked at his alarm clock and wondered why it had not rung. "Oh, yes! It is Saturday, no school today!" he cried as he leaped out of his bed.

Peering out a clear spot the frosty window, Marcus noticed his neighbor was trying to walk toward the mailbox. It was so deep, his neighbor, Mr. Ambrosia, looked like he was wading through a mound of sticky cotton. Marcus decided to shovel the walkway. He put on his coat and hurried outside.

After shoveling the walk, Marcus came inside. He noticed his new sled in the hall. Mom and Dad had given Marcus and Seth a matching pair for their birthday a few days ago. "Make sure you put these on so your heads will stay warm," said Mom, handing something to each boy as he walked through the front door. The boys were off to the city park. They had a great time racing their new sleds down the hill. The cold wind numbed their faces as they slid swiftly through the snow. The boys were glad that Mom reminded them to wear their winter gear. They remained comfortable the whole time they were sledding.

Upon returning home, they smelled something sweet. It reminded the boys of cinnamon sticks and sugar. Mom had been baking all afternoon. They saw some round, soft circles on the cooling rack. Best of all, some were left on a plate for the boys. Marcus and Seth rushed to the table and ate all of them quickly. "This is great!" they exclaimed. "What a super way to end the day!" The boys decided today was the best day yet.

Step 2 Student Tips

To infer from the story, you need to remember:

- There are clues in the story. Clues are hints the author gives you about the story. Draw a line under each clue, or use your finger to point to the clue.

- What you know will help you figure out the story. Think about what is going on in the story. Have you done it before? Do you know about it?

- Clues, experiences, and knowledge are put together.

- Using clues from the the story and what you know will help you figure out what is happening in the story. (This is called an **inference**.)

Step 3 Complete the reading map. Use the reading map to help you think about inferring.

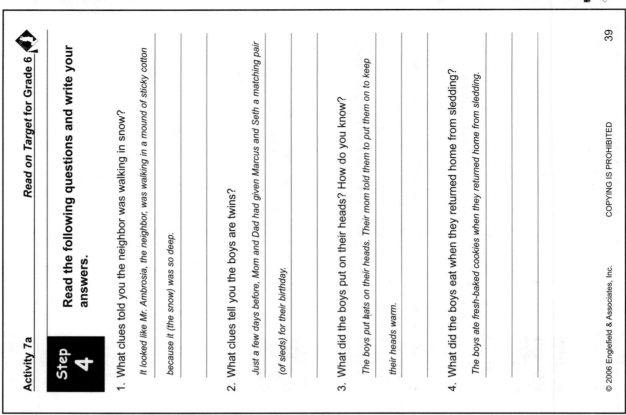

Read on Target for Grade 6

Activity 7a

Step 4

Read the following questions and write your answers.

1. What clues told you the neighbor was walking in snow?

   It looked like Mr. Ambrosia, the neighbor, was walking in a mound of sticky cotton

   because it (the snow) was so deep.

2. What clues tell you the boys are twins?

   Just a few days before, Mom and Dad had given Marcus and Seth a matching pair

   (of sleds) for their birthday.

3. What did the boys put on their heads? How do you know?

   The boys put hats on their heads. Their mom told them to put them on to keep

   their heads warm.

4. What did the boys eat when they returned home from sledding?

   The boys ate fresh-baked cookies when they returned home from sledding.

39

© 2006 Englefield & Associates, Inc.   COPYING IS PROHIBITED

Note: Student answers may vary. Example responses in italics are for use as a guide.

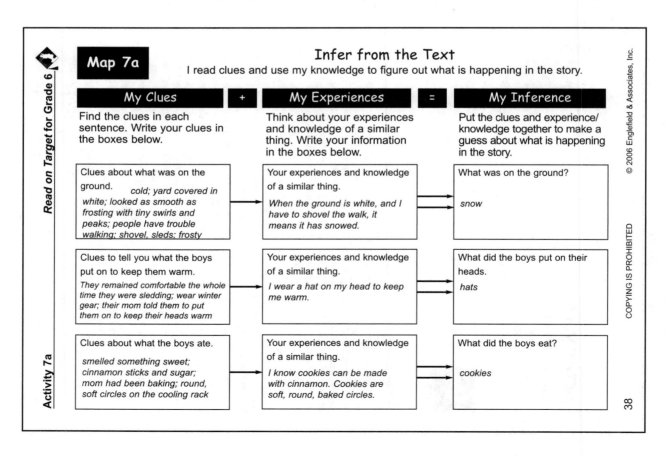

Map 7a

Infer from the Text
I read clues and use my knowledge to figure out what is happening in the story.

My Clues	+	My Experiences	=	My Inference
Find the clues in each sentence. Write your clues in the boxes below.		Think about your experiences and knowledge of a similar thing. Write your information in the boxes below.		Put the clues and experience/knowledge together to make a guess about what is happening in the story.

Clues about what was on the ground. *cold; yard covered in white; looked as smooth as frosting with tiny swirls and peaks; people have trouble walking; shovel, sleds; frosty* → Your experiences and knowledge of a similar thing. *When the ground is white, and I have to shovel the walk, it means it has snowed.* → What was on the ground? *snow*

Clues to tell you what the boys put on to keep them warm. *They remained comfortable the whole time they were sledding; wear winter gear; their mom told them to put them on to keep their heads warm* → Your experiences and knowledge of a similar thing. *I wear a hat on my head to keep me warm.* → What did the boys put on their heads. *hats*

Clues about what the boys ate. *smelled something sweet; cinnamon sticks and sugar; mom had been baking; round, soft circles on the cooling rack* → Your experiences and knowledge of a similar thing. *I know cookies can be made with cinnamon. Cookies are soft, round, baked circles.* → What did the boys eat? *cookies*

Activity 7a   38

© 2006 Englefield & Associates, Inc.   COPYING IS PROHIBITED

Activity 7b

Infer from the Text

I read clues and use what I know to figure out what is happening in the story.

Step 1 Read the story "Away From Home."

Away From Home

Our car drove down the winding lane, through the woods, past the swimming pool, and finally around the lake. We passed many groups of cabins, soccer and baseball fields, and even a giant tree swing. After we finally came to a stop, I opened the car door and slowly picked up my sleeping bag and suitcase. "Bye Mom," I said with a frown. This was my first time away from home. Even worse, I had to leave my most treasured possession behind: my bike!

"Have a wonderful time, and don't forget to write," said Mom. I watched as the car slowly crept back down the lane. Unfamiliar kids were everywhere, hurrying and laughing with one another, carrying their bags and suitcases into the different cabins that surrounded the area. My legs felt like wood as I made my way slowly to Cabin 4, a building I would have to call home for the next two weeks whether I liked it or not.

My sleeping bag felt heavy in my arms. I knew I was not supposed to cry, but I just couldn't help it. I had never been away from home. This was my first time at this place. I did not know if I could get used to the idea of spending two whole weeks away from home, away from my bike, and with so many strangers!

As I walked shaking like a leaf through the cabin door, two people looked at me. They sat quietly and looked just the way I felt. We all turned around as we saw a woman walk through the door and into our cabin. "This must be our cabin leader," I thought to myself.

"Hi, I am Juanita," said the woman as she approached the three of us. "You must be Jane, Carol, and Marci," she added. "It is time to check out the activities. Follow me." She smiled warmly.

As we strolled around, Juanita showed us all of the highlights. First, she showed us all the different sports fields. There were fields for baseball, soccer, and football as well as a big open area for whatever game we could think of to amuse ourselves. She told us any equipment we needed was kept in the building where we would be eating our meals. She also pointed out many different trails which could be used for hiking or any other purpose. She then took us by the lake and showed us the area that had been roped off for swimming. It even had a rope swing to jump off the dock! Next to the lake was a shed. As we approached it, Juanita explained to us that some equipment, such as canoes for the lake, were too big to be kept anywhere else, so a shed was built for them. As Juanita opened the shed to display its contents, my heart skipped a beat as some of the equipment caught my eye. They were shiny, new, and looked to be just the right size. I started to smile, as did my two cabin mates.

Then we were off down the dirt trails Juanita had shown us earlier! I was on the red and gold racer with red handlebars. I quickly turned out of sight. As we came around the bend, Juanita let out a cry and cheered us on. Carol pulled in front of us and raced to the front of the line. Soon, Marci pulled up to the lead. We had a great time no matter who was in front.

We returned to the cabin and unpacked our bags. I heard a friendly voice in the bunk next to mine ask, "Hi, Jane, want to ride later?" It was Carol.

Smiling, I said, "I would love to."

Map 7b

Infer from the Text
I read clues and use my knowledge to figure out what is happening in the story.

My Clues	+	My Experiences	=	My Inference
Find the clues in each sentence. Write your clues in the boxes below.		Think about your experiences and knowledge of a similar thing. Write your information in the boxes below.		Put the clues and experience/knowledge together to make a guess about what is happening in the story.

Clues to tell you where Jane is.

winding lake; past the swimming pool; sleeping bags & suitcase; cabin; away from home for two weeks

→ Your experiences and knowledge of a similar thing.

We use sleeping bags and tents to camp overnight.

→ Where is Jane?

Jane is at camp.

Clues to tell you what she rode.

wide dirt trail; shiny and red

→ Your experiences and knowledge of a similar thing.

I ride my bike on a dirt trail. I have seen a shiny, red bike.

→ What did she ride?

a bike

Clues to tell you what Jane's final attitude is about camp.

smile; friendly voice; had a great time

→ Your experiences and knowledge of a similar thing.

I am happy and smiling when I am enjoying something.

→ Is Jane enjoying camp?

Yes, she made friends and found a bike to ride.

Note: Student answers may vary. Example responses in italics are for use as a guide.

Step 2 — Student Tips

To infer from the story, you need to remember:

* There are clues in the story. Clues are hints the author gives you about the story. Draw a line under each clue, or use your finger to point to the clue.
* What you know will help you figure out the story. Think about what is going on in the story. Have you done it before? Do you know about it?
* Clues, experiences, and knowledge are put together.
* Using clues from the the story and what you know will help you figure out what is happening in the story. (This is called an **inference.**)

Step 3

Complete the reading map. Use the reading map to help you think about inferring.

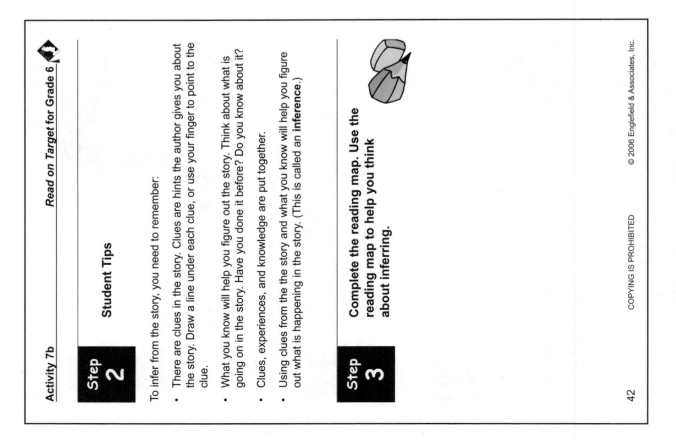

Note: Student answers may vary. Example responses in italics are for use as a guide.

Read on Target for Grade 6

Activity 7b

Step 4

Read the following questions and write your answers.

1. Where is Jane? What clues told you where Jane is?

   Jane is at camp. I knew she was at camp because she had her sleeping bag and a

   suitcase. A cabin was mentioned. Also, she said she was going to be away from

   home for two weeks.

2. What is Jane riding on the trail? What clues helped you figure it out?

   Jane is riding a bike on the trail. I knew she was on a bike because the story

   mentioned it was shiny and red and was able to travel along a dirt trail.

3. How did you figure out if Jane is enjoying camp?

   She found a bike and her cabinmate Carol asks her to ride later. She smiled and

   agreed.

4. What is your experience or knowledge that helped you figure out what Jane rode?

   Answers should match the student's response from the "My Experiences" boxes on

   Reading Map 7b.

44　　COPYING IS PROHIBITED　　© 2006 Englefield & Associates, Inc.

Troubleshooting: Understanding Inference

The first problem that students need to overcome in understanding inference is comprehending what the term "infer" means. They simply are unfamiliar with what inferring really is. Before using the reading map, teachers must make it clear to students that if a statement appears in the text, it CANNOT be an inference. They also need to know that they make inferences every day by observing and then drawing from previous knowledge. This skill then becomes much less abstract for them.

Students often know how to infer but are not aware that they already know how to do it. For example, if Johnny sees Tommy run into the classroom, throw down his books on the floor, and become very red in the face, Johnny makes the inference that Tommy is upset about something. He doesn't think about the process he followed of making observations of Tommy's actions and then accessing his previous knowledge of similar experiences to make the inference. The same is true in reading. The student reads the facts in the text, draws on prior knowledge, and then makes an inference. Again, the key is if the statement can be found in the text, it is NOT an inference; rather, it is a clue. If students understand this simple concept, they won't make the common mistake of giving textual information as an inference.

When they have absorbed the fact that inferences will not be found in the text, it is much easier for them to follow the procedures to make inferences. Younger students will see this as making a guess from what they know, and older students may see this as drawing a conclusion, but it is important for them to understand the parts of the process in order to evaluate whether or not their inferences are logical and why.

After reading the text, students must first locate the clues in the story that lead them to make their inferences. Then they should think about the personal experiences they draw upon in order to formulate their inferences. By focusing on this process, students begin to understand there is a logic implied in making an inference, and they can actually have a point of reference in understanding why their analyses are reasonable or not reasonable. Surprisingly, this can be a kind of "Aha!" experience for students. Your more able students may have already understood this, but you will have a significant number of students who have never given thought to the process at all.

This technique is an equally effective application in both fiction and nonfiction text. Using this process can lead to much better reasoning in understanding character, setting, making predictions, etc. It can also help students to see the logic or lack of logic in evaluating persuasive writing.

8

Predict from the Text

Teaching Tips

What Do Students Need to Know?

Making predictions gives students opportunities to connect information in the story with experiences and knowledge to anticipate **what will happen next**. The more experiences students have in predicting, the more likely they are to think about the possibilities that could happen given a set of events. Students develop predicting skills by **reading clues** from the story and using their **knowledge** and **experiences** to figure out what will happen next. Students need varied experiences. Oftentimes they do not have opportunities or experiences to process the information required for predicting. To assist students in developing a broader base of information, teachers may need to provide real-life experiences, discussion, or pictures that correlate with the information in the story. For example, before reading a story about the beach, provide materials that are found at the beach. Teachers may want to bring beach materials such as sand, shells, or pictures of a beach into the classroom before reading a story about the beach. Students need to be questioned about their experiences during the guided-instruction phase of completing the prediction map. To increase an understanding of the clues, teachers need to point to the title and ask students what the story is about. In addition, teachers can identify a clue from the book and ask why it is a clue, or how the clue helped students make a guess about what is happening in the story. This focuses students on the demands of clues, experiences, and knowledge.

Use of the Reading Maps

When students predict, they often use the beginning and middle of a story to help figure out what will happen at the end. As students continue to read, they find more clues and use experiences and prior knowledge to include or to exclude from their predictions or guesses about what will happen next.

The reading map will guide students to:

- Read the sentence or paragraph to find clues about the meaning of the story.

- Write the clues in the box.

- Write about an experience or knowledge of a similar thing.

- Put together clues and experience or knowledge to make a prediction about what will happen next.

- Read more of the story to see if the prediction is supported by the additional clues, repeat Steps 2–4.

Second Prediction Question: A skateboarder is coming down the hill at a fast speed. Her skateboard runs off the bike trail and hits a wall of stone. What happens to the skateboard?

Third Prediction Question: A boy on in-line skates is on the bike path. He is coming down the hill. He applies his brakes in a sudden motion. What happens to the person on in-line skates?

Keesha recorded her observations on a prediction chart and wondered what would happen in the future if someone ran into a pothole that was on the bike path. She thought a good scientist would use observations as one way to think about what might happen in the future. Keesha planned to continue to use observation as a method of scientific investigation.

Activity 8a

Predict from the Text

I read clues and use my knowledge to figure out what will happen in the future.

Step 1   Read the passage "The Bike Trail."

The Bike Trail

Keesha had been thinking about becoming a scientist when she is older. Keesha had learned in science class that something will stay in motion until an opposing force causes it to stop. She thought about making observations and making predictions based upon her observations. She also thought her observations would help her figure out what might happen in the future when a similar thing occurs. She decided to practice collecting data based on her observations. One day after school, she sat in the cool shade under a tree while watching kids on bikes, skateboards, and inline skates. Keesha saw a bike rider run into a pothole. He came to a sudden stop. His helmet fell forward. Based on her observations and knowledge, Keesha wrote some prediction questions.

First Prediction Question: A girl with a long ponytail is riding her bike. The ponytail is pointing out straight behind her back as she rides. The bike suddenly stops. What happens to her ponytail?

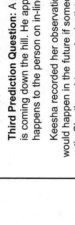

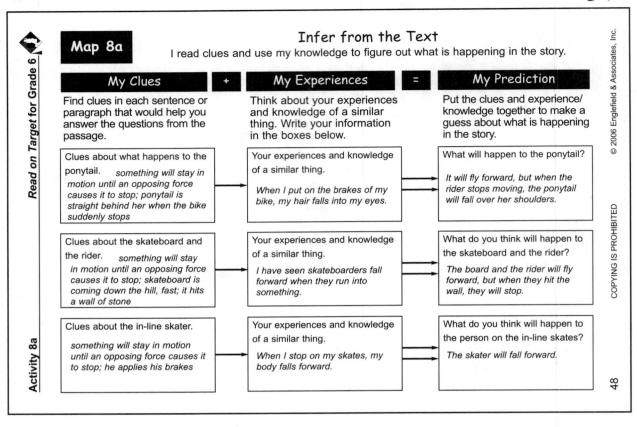

Note: Student answers may vary. Example responses in italics are for use as a guide.

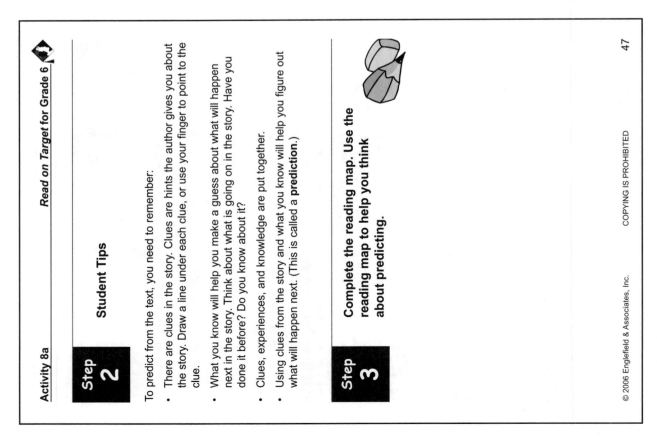

Activity 8b

Predict from the Text

I read clues and use my knowledge to figure out what will happen in the future.

© 2006 Englefield & Associates, Inc.

| Step 1 | **Read the information in "A Day at the Beach."** |

A Day at the Beach

On Friday, Jordan and her brother, Michael, pack their bags. They are ready to go to Grandmother and Grandfather's beach house for a week-long summer vacation. Both children are excited to see the crystal blue water and golden sand. They always get up early and go to bed late because there are so many activities to do at the beach. They enjoy fishing, making sandcastles, and swimming in the ocean.

Each of them has a new activity to try on this vacation. Michael's new activity is surfing. Michael wants to learn how to surf on his new, bright, shiny board. He loves the thought of surfing when the wave action is fast and furious. He knows the best time to surf is at high tide.

Jordan would like to collect unusual seashells. She has collected seashells before, but this year, she hopes to find many different kinds of shells on the beach.

Note: Student answers may vary. Example responses in italics are for use as a guide.

| Step 4 | **Read the following questions and write your answers.** |

1. What do you think will happen to the skateboard and the rider?

   The skateboard and the rider will fly forward until they hit the wall. When they hit

   the wall, they will stop moving.

2. How did you figure out the answer to question 1?

   Students should use the information from the "My Experiences" boxes on Reading

   Map 8a to answer this question.

3. What do you think will happen to the person on the in-line skates?

   The person will fall forward when the brakes are used.

4. What clues from the passage helped you figure out what happens to the girl's ponytail after the bike suddenly stops?

   Something will stay in motion until an opposing force causes it to stop. The ponytail

   is pointing straight behind the rider. When the bike stops, motion stops, so the

   ponytail will fall onto the rider's shoulders.

Activity 8b   *Read on Target* for Grade 6

Step 2

Student Tips

To predict from the text, you need to remember:

- There are clues in the story. Clues are hints the author gives you about the story. Draw a line under each clue, or use your finger to point to the clue.

- What you know will help you make a guess about what will happen next in the story. Think about what is going on in the story. Have you done it before? Do you know about it?

- Clues, experiences, and knowledge are put together.

- Using clues from the story and what you know will help you figure out what will happen next. (This is called a **prediction**.)

Step 3

Complete the reading map. Use the reading map to help you think about predicting.

52   © 2006 Englefield & Associates, Inc.

Activity 8b   *Read on Target* for Grade 6

Jordan found an old chart in the living room. It listed the schedule of the tides. The schedule was for last week, the week before they arrived at the beach. They think there is enough information in the chart that will give clues to tell them when the tides will be low and high during the week of their vacation. Low tide is when the water recedes and more land is exposed, and the water is calmer at low tide. High tide is when the water reaches its highest point and covers the most land. At high tide, the big waves crash one after another. Here is what part of the tide chart looked like.

	Monday	Tuesday	Wednesday	Thursday	Friday
Low Tide	5:04 a.m.	5:09 a.m.	5:15 a.m.	5:22 a.m.	5:30 a.m.
High Tide	3:02 p.m.	3:10 p.m.	3:19 p.m.	3:29 p.m.	3:40 p.m.

© 2006 Englefield & Associates, Inc.   COPYING IS PROHIBITED   51

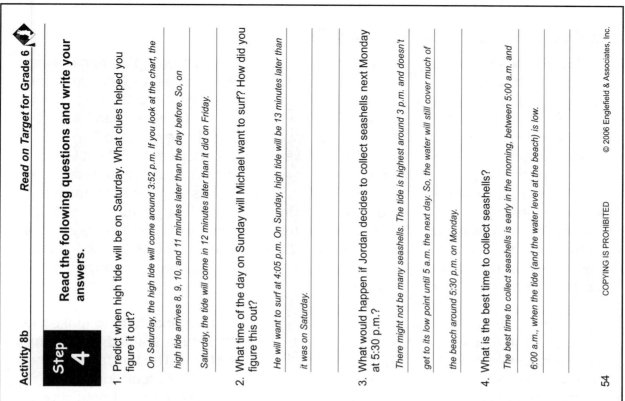

Step 4

Read the following questions and write your answers.

1. Predict when high tide will be on Saturday. What clues helped you figure it out?

On Saturday, the high tide will come around 3:52 p.m. If you look at the chart, the

high tide arrives 8, 9, 10, and 11 minutes later than the day before. So, on

Saturday, the tide will come in 12 minutes later than it did on Friday.

2. What time of the day on Sunday will Michael want to surf? How did you figure this out?

He will want to surf at 4:05 p.m. On Sunday, high tide will be 13 minutes later than

it was on Saturday.

3. What would happen if Jordan decides to collect seashells next Monday at 5:30 p.m.?

There might not be many seashells. The tide is highest around 3 p.m. and doesn't

get to its low point until 5 a.m. the next day. So, the water will still cover much of

the beach around 5:30 p.m. on Monday.

4. What is the best time to collect seashells?

The best time to collect seashells is early in the morning, between 5:00 a.m. and

6:00 a.m., when the tide (and the water level at the beach) is low.

54   © 2006 Englefield & Associates, Inc.   COPYING IS PROHIBITED

Note: Student answers may vary. Example responses in italics are for use as a guide.

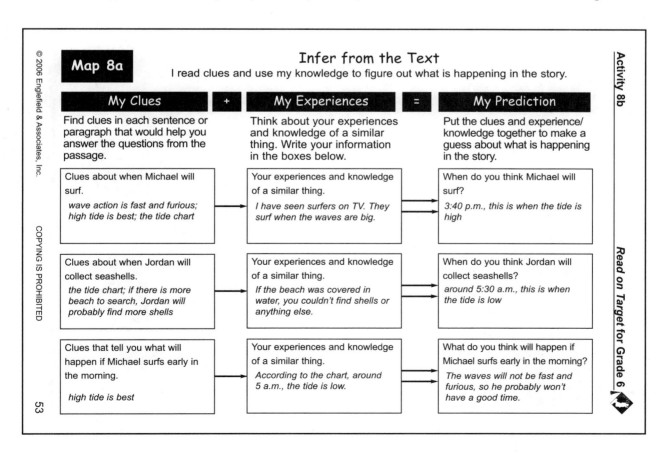

Map 8a

Infer from the Text
I read clues and use my knowledge to figure out what is happening in the story.

My Clues	+	My Experiences	=	My Prediction
Find clues in each sentence or paragraph that would help you answer the questions from the passage.		Think about your experiences and knowledge of a similar thing. Write your information in the boxes below.		Put the clues and experience/knowledge together to make a guess about what is happening in the story.

Clues about when Michael will surf.	Your experiences and knowledge of a similar thing.	When do you think Michael will surf?
wave action is fast and furious; high tide is best; the tide chart	*I have seen surfers on TV. They surf when the waves are big.*	*3:40 p.m., this is when the tide is high*

Clues about when Jordan will collect seashells.	Your experiences and knowledge of a similar thing.	When do you think Jordan will collect seashells?
the tide chart; if there is more beach to search, Jordan will probably find more shells	*If the beach was covered in water, you couldn't find shells or anything else.*	*around 5:30 a.m., this is when the tide is low*

Clues that tell you what will happen if Michael surfs early in the morning.	Your experiences and knowledge of a similar thing.	What do you think will happen if Michael surfs early in the morning?
high tide is best	*According to the chart, around 5 a.m., the tide is low.*	*The waves will not be fast and furious, so he probably won't have a good time.*

Troubleshooting: Understanding Predicting

The skill of predicting is very similar to making inferences, the only difference being that the reader is making an inference about what will happen rather than what has already happened. Predicting is a skill that readers do as a process of being an engaged reader. In predicting, readers are validated by continuing to read the text to find out if their mental predictions were correct. Some readers even take it to the extreme by reading the end of the selection first because they cannot stand the suspense of reading everything in between to find out if their predictions were correct. On the other hand, poor readers do not make predictions as they read; consequently, they are not engaged in their reading enough to care to continue to read ahead. It is these readers who will need daily practice in using this process. Engaged readers are already doing it, even though they may not realize they are. These students can be valuable assets in helping their classmates to understand the process, once they understand they are already predicting.

As in inferring, students must identify the clues in the text that led them to make their predictions. They must also understand the previous knowledge that led them to make their predictions in order to justify the logic of their predictions. The validation of the process is the reading ahead to see if they were correct in their predictions. It is important for students to know that it is not a mistake to make incorrect predictions as long as they have a clear, logical basis for making them.

9

Compare and Contrast

Teaching Tips

What Do Students Need to Know?

Students need to understand how two or more things are **alike** and **different**. After reading the text, students will begin to connect the information they read to their experiences and will gain an understanding of how things are related. Oftentimes, students will need to make these connections by determining what the information does or does not have in common with something else. Students will need to be able to describe the characteristics of what they are going to compare and contrast. Next, they need to determine if the characteristics of the items are alike or different.

Use of the Reading Map

The use of this map will provide opportunities for students to describe the characteristics of the items and determine if these items have qualities that are alike or different from each other. Students will have a visual picture of items compared and contrasted by describing the characteristics or attributes. Next, students will determine if these characteristics or attributes are alike or different.

The reading map will guide students to:

- Write the names of the things to be compared and contrasted in the shaded boxes.

- Describe the characteristics of the things to be compared and contrasted. A blank box is provided for students to write their own characteristics to be compared and contrasted.

- If the items have the **same** characteristic, circle the plus sign (+) in the box under the shaded boxes and next to the "Describe the Characteristic" box.

- If the items have **different** characteristics, circle the minus sign (–) in the box under the shaded boxes and next to the "Describe the Characteristic" box.

- Now, students are ready to write what things are the same and different.

Activity 9a

Compare and Contrast

I read to find out how two or more things are alike and different.

Step 1   **Read the article "Frogs and Toads."**

Frogs and Toads

It's important to look closely to see if the animal you are about to kiss is a frog or a toad. After all, a girl may never find a handsome prince if she kisses the wrong amphibian. Can you tell the difference between a frog and a toad?

At first glance, it may be easy to confuse frogs and toads. They are both amphibians. This means they can live both in water and on land. They both are coldblooded. This means their body temperatures are the same as the air temperature around them. They have to look for cool, shady places to rest if they become too hot. Frogs and toads look for warm, sunny places if they are too cold. Both animals are vertebrates, which means they have backbones. Their basic body shape is similar. Their eyes bulge out from their faces, so they can see in most directions without turning their heads. Frogs and toads use their long, sticky tongues to catch insects to eat. Both frogs and toads swallow their food whole.

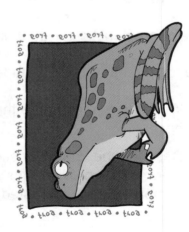

55

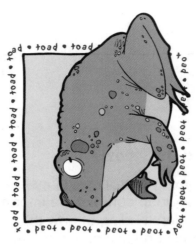

With all of these similarities, how are frogs and toads different? Frogs are better swimmers and jumpers, because they have long, muscular back legs. A toad's back legs are usually shorter. Frogs are more likely to be found near water, while toads often visit drier places. Most frogs have four webbed feet, but toads do not have webs on their back feet. The skin of a frog is smooth and slightly damp. Toads usually have drier skin that is covered with bumps called glands. Frogs have teeth in their upper jaw and rarely have teeth in their lower jaws. Toads have no teeth at all.

As you can see, frogs and toads are not the same amphibian. Of course, a frog turning into a handsome prince only happens in fairy tales. Who would want to kiss a frog or a toad anyway?

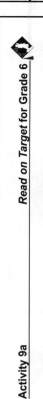

Map 9a

Compare and Contrast
I read to figure out how two things are alike and different.

Directions: How would you describe the things that you are going to compare and contrast? What shape are they? What color are they? Circle the plus sign (+) in a box if the items are similar. Circle the minus sign (–) in a box if the items are different.

Describe the Characteristics. Tell what the things look like. Write your answer in the box next to these characteristics. (Under the shaded boxes.)	Write the names of the things that you are going to compare and contrast in the two shaded boxes below.		
	frog		toad
Shape	bulging eyes; 4 legs	⊕ or –	bulging eyes; 4 legs
Color	X	+ or –	X
Size	long back legs	+ or ⊖	short back legs
It is. . .	amphibian: coldblooded; vertebrate	⊕ or –	amphibian: coldblooded; vertebrate
Sounds like. . .	X	+ or –	X
Feels like. . .	slightly damp skin, smooth	+ or ⊖	dry skin, bumpy
Write your own characteristic to compare and contrast.			
teeth	in upper jaw	+ or ⊖	no teeth

© 2006 Englefield & Associates, Inc.

COPYING IS PROHIBITED

Activity 9a

58

Note: Student answers may vary. Example responses in italics are for use as a guide.

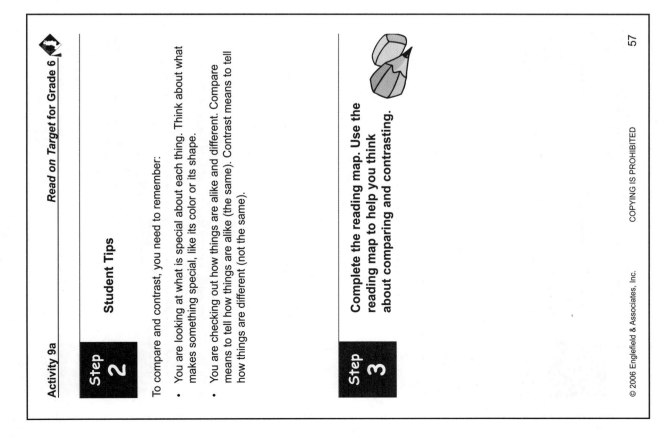

Step 2

Student Tips

To compare and contrast, you need to remember:

- You are looking at what is special about each thing. Think about what makes something special, like its color or its shape.

- You are checking out how things are alike and different. Compare means to tell how things are alike (the same). Contrast means to tell how things are different (not the same).

Step 3

Complete the reading map. Use the reading map to help you think about comparing and contrasting.

© 2006 Englefield & Associates, Inc.

COPYING IS PROHIBITED

Activity 9b

Compare and Contrast

I read to find out how two or more things are alike and different.

Step 1   **Read the story "Apples and Oranges."**

Apples and Oranges

My cousins Nikki and Logan are twins. You would think they would be just alike, but they are fraternal twins. That means although they were born at the same time, they do not share the exact same features. Twins who look exactly alike are called identical twins. We like to call Nikki and Logan "apples and oranges" because although they may be twins, they are not alike.

They do look a bit alike, considering that one is a boy and the other is a girl. They are both 5 feet tall. Their noses and mouths are the same shapes as their father's. Our grandmother used to call it an Irish lip. We never quite understood what that meant. Nikki has curly auburn hair and hazel eyes, and Logan has dark brown hair and very dark brown eyes. But their voices and facial expressions brand them as brother and sister, which they hate when people make mention of it.

When it comes to hobbies, that is where Nikki and Logan can really be called "apples and oranges." Nikki likes ballet and enjoys curling up alone with a good book. Logan, on the other hand, enjoys playing football and other sports. He enjoys spending his time with his friends outside. Nikki enjoys going to school, and her favorite part of school is art class. Logan does not like going to school. His favorite part of school is recess.

Nikki and Logan seem to fight constantly. When our family is together for holidays and special occasions, they always pick at and tease each other until the squawking becomes full blown. They always seem to end up "in the doghouse." I think the reason why they fight so much is they are competing for attention. Maybe it's because they are twins, and they have had to share a lot.

60   COPYING IS PROHIBITED   © 2006 Englefield & Associates, Inc.

Note: Student answers may vary. Example responses in italics are for use as a guide.

Activity 9a

Step 4   **Read the following questions and write your answers.**

1. Frogs and toads are what type of animal?

Frogs and toads are both amphibians.

2. In what ways are frogs and toads different?

A toad's back legs are shorter than a frog's. Toads live in drier areas than frogs.

3. How are the body structures of frogs and toads alike?

Frogs and toads both have four legs and bulging eyes. They are also similar in

shape.

4. Frogs and toads eat in a similar way. Identify this similarity.

They both use their long, sticky tongues to catch food. They also both swallow their

food whole.

© 2006 Englefield & Associates, Inc.   COPYING IS PROHIBITED   59

Activity 9b   *Read on Target* for Grade 6

Step 2

Student Tips

To compare and contrast, you need to remember:

- You are looking at what is special about each thing. Think about what makes something special, like its color or its shape.

- You are checking out how things are alike and different. Compare means to tell how things are alike (the same). Contrast means to tell how things are different (not the same).

Step 3

Complete the reading map. Use the reading map to help you think about comparing and contrasting.

Activity 9b   *Read on Target* for Grade 6

One day on a family vacation, they were fighting so loudly, their parents came in from fishing out on the lake. Aunt Michelle and Uncle Dave said they could hear Nikki bellowing at Logan all the way out at their favorite perch hole. They came roaring in and told Nikki and Logan to go up to their rooms for the rest of the afternoon. We were all kind of sad because we had planned to have a water-basketball game and needed two more players to make up our teams. Nikki and Logan are both great water-basketball players. Neither one lets anyone get near the basket we have rigged up on the dock.

Nikki and Logan grudgingly left the dock, both blaming each other for getting themselves punished. Nikki slammed the door to the girls' bunkroom, and Logan did the same to the boys' side. We tried to get the water-basketball game under way without them, but it just wasn't the same without the two most aggressive players. Besides, we only had four people to play with instead of six. Finally, we called it quits and went up to the bunkrooms to get out of our wet bathing suits.

Nikki and Logan were in the girls' bunkroom talking and watching a movie together. When they saw us, Logan just smiled and Nikki grinned. I don't think they want us to know how much they really like each other. We just looked at each other, scratching our heads. I guess sometimes apples and oranges can come together to make a pretty good fruit salad!

Read on Target for Grade 6

Activity 9b

Step 4

Read the following questions and write your answers.

1. In the story, Nikki and Logan are twins. Tell some ways they are similar.

   Their noses and mouths are both like their father's. They are both 5 feet tall. They have similar voices and facial expressions. They are both good water-basketball players. They both pick at and tease each other.

2. Explain some ways the twins are different.

   Nikki has curly, auburn hair, while Logan has dark brown hair. Nikki's eyes are hazel, and Logan's eyes are brown. Nikki likes school, but Logan does not. Nikki is a girl. Logan is a boy.

3. Compare Logan and Nikki to other twins you have known. Are they similar to or different from other twins?

   Student responses will vary.

4. Decide whether you believe Logan and Nikki are more the same or more different. Give examples from the text to support your opinion.

   They are more similar because the reading map shows more "+" symbols.

64

Note: Student answers may vary. Example responses in italics are for use as a guide.

Activity 9b

Read on Target for Grade 6

Map 9a

Compare and Contrast
I read to figure out how two things are alike and different.

Directions: How would you describe the things that you are going to compare and contrast? What shape are they? What color are they? Circle the plus sign (+) in a box if the items are similar. Circle the minus sign (–) in a box if the items are different.

Describe the Characteristics. Tell what the things look like. Write your answer in the box next to these characteristics. (Under the shaded boxes.)	Write the names of the things that you are going to compare and contrast in the two shaded boxes below.		
	Nikki		Logan
Shape	expressions, nose, mouth	⊕ or –	expressions, nose, mouth
Color	hazel eyes, curly auburn hair	+ or ⊖	dark brown eyes and hair
Size	5 feet tall	⊕ or –	5 feet tall
It is. . .	girl	+ or ⊖	boy
Sounds like. . .	squawking voices	⊕ or –	squawking voices
Feels like. . .	X	+ or –	X
Write your own characteristic to compare and contrast.			
behavior	fighting, teasing, squawking, slamming door, attention	⊕ or –	fighting, teasing, squawking, slamming door, attention

Troubleshooting: Understanding Comparing and Contrasting

The most common breakdown that students have in understanding how to compare and contrast is that they do not completely address the topic. Using a chart such as the reading map will help students formulate clear and complete ideas on showing differences and similarities between characters, scientific elements, U.S. Presidents, or even math formulas. The operative words here are: similarities, differences, and complete.

A comparison/contrast response should also be balanced. If I say that, unlike a snail, a slug is soft-bodied, I also need to state that the snail is a soft-bodied animal that develops a hard outer coating to protect itself. Students should be able to draw from the text at least two separate ways a topic is similar or different and be able to support their examples from the text.

A helpful exercise is to give students two objects. Ask them to list as many things about them that are similar and that are different. The tricky part is to get the students to put their lists into balanced sentences that reflect similarity-to-similarity, or difference-to-difference. Using a chart or a list will point them in the right direction.

Example:

Items	Similarities	Differences
Red ball	round, warm color, can be held, leathery texture	red, non-living, toy, can be played with
Orange	round, warm color, can be held, leathery texture	orange, living, fruit, can be eaten

Although a red ball is round, has a warm color, and is leathery in texture like an orange, the red ball is really a different color than the orange. The ball was never alive like the orange. Their surfaces are different. The ball is meant to be played with; the fruit is meant to be eaten. Even though the ball and orange may look vaguely similar, they are two completely different things.

10 Analyze the Text by Examining the Use of Fact and Opinion

Teaching Tips

What Do Students Need to Know?

Students need to be able to determine if the information in the text is something that **can be proven** or is **a personal belief**. When students read to analyze whether or not the information is a **fact**, they need to decide if the information can be proven by evidence or observation, can be checked by looking up the information in a book such as an encyclopedia, and if it is true for everyone. An **opinion** tells how someone thinks or feels about something. Students might agree or disagree with an opinion. When reading information, students need to separate facts from opinions. Some key words give clues as to whether a statement is a fact or an opinion. These key words are clues that tell how a person thinks or feels about something. Key words can also be words that make something greater than it is, such as an exaggeration. An exaggeration overstates the way a person feels or thinks. When added to a sentence, a key word can change the meaning of that sentence from a fact to an opinion. By practicing changing facts to opinion and vice versa, students are able to recognize fact and opinion when presented in nonfiction.

Use of the Reading Maps

When students analyze fact and opinion, they first read the text. Next, they determine if the information is based on evidence and can be proven, or if it is a personal belief that is based on how someone feels or thinks or is a judgment. Key words may provide clues for students to help indicate whether the statement is a fact or an opinion. Prior to using the reading map, the fact and opinion student worksheet will provide students practice determining key words that indicate an opinion. The worksheet will also provide practice in writing fact and opinion sentences. After using the student worksheet, students will be better prepared to complete the reading map.

The reading map will guide students to:

- Write a sentence or sentences from the text that tell if the story is a fact or an opinion.

- Determine how the sentences are supported by facts or opinions.

COPYING IS PROHIBITED

- If the sentences tell that the reading material is a fact then:

  1. Write how the information can be proven by evidence or observation.

  2. Write where you would look up the information or where you would see it.

  3. Tell if the information is true for everyone.

- If the sentences tell that the reading material is an opinion then:

  1. Write KEY WORDS that are clues to tell how someone thinks or feels.

  2. Write how the information tells a personal belief or judgment about something.

  3. Tell if the information is true for some people.

Activity 10a

Analyze the Text by Examining the Use of Fact and Opinion

I figure out if the sentence can be proven or is a personal belief that tells how someone feels or thinks.

Step 1 Read the story "Washington, D.C."

Washington, D.C.

Our family went to Washington, D.C., for a week-long family trip at our nation's capital. Everyone loves Washington, D.C., because it is the only city in the United States that is not located in a state. I found it interesting that this city is the center of government in the United States. It is the capital of the United States. Washington, D.C., is a symbol of our country's history and tradition; consequently, it is a site of many popular tourist attractions.

The states of Maryland and Virginia border Washington, D.C. I saw the Potomac River to the west and south of the city. I was surprised to learn that this city is at least 69 square miles in size. Washington, D.C., seemed packed full of people. It is one of the more densely populated cities in the United States.

Some people go there to see senators, representatives, and, sometimes, the President. We were able to observe Congress in session. Watching government in action is exciting. This is the city where most of the federal employees work; thousands of people work in Washington, D.C. We were hoping to see the most important federal employee, the President.

Many people visit Washington, D.C. They go there to see government buildings, monuments, and other famous tourist attractions. Some of the sites I saw were the Lincoln Memorial, the Washington Monument, Ford's Theater, and the White House. We also visited a beautiful park with many blossoming cherry trees. Just imagine enjoying a large garden oasis right next to a bustling city.

Activity 10a

The Lincoln Memorial is a stately white building that has a statue of President Abraham Lincoln sitting on a chair. Paintings and quotations from Lincoln were in the monument. It was very impressive. My favorite site, though, was the Washington Monument. When I went inside, I got on an elevator that whisked me to the very top. Because it is the tallest structure in Washington, D.C., I could see the whole city from the top of the monument. What a spectacular sight. After visiting the Washington Monument, we moved on to the White House. It was quite crowded but definitely worth the visit. I was able to tour several rooms such as the Red Room and the Blue Room with their magnificent works of art. At our last stop, Ford's Theater, we were able to tour the building where Abraham Lincoln was assassinated.

It was a busy week in Washington, D.C. I learned so much visiting various government sites. I think everyone would love to visit Washington, D.C., and would be fortunate to have an opportunity to visit our capital.

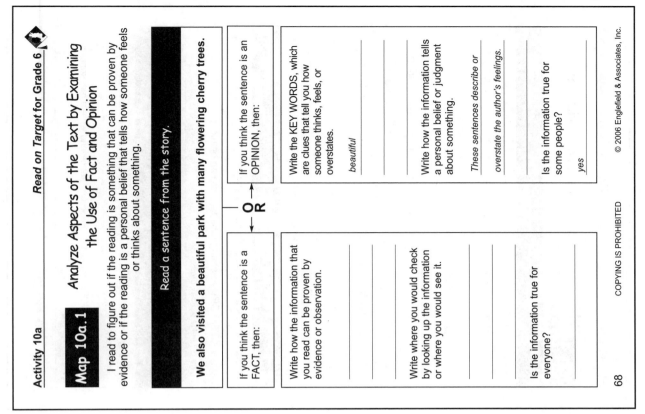

Activity 10a   *Read on Target for Grade 6*

Map 10a.1 — Analyze Aspects of the Text by Examining the Use of Fact and Opinion

I read to figure out if the reading is something that can be proven by evidence or if the reading is a personal belief that tells how someone feels or thinks about something.

Read a sentence from the story.

We also visited a beautiful park with many flowering cherry trees.

OR

If you think the sentence is a FACT, then:

Write how the information that you read can be proven by evidence or observation.

Write where you would check by looking up the information or where you would see it.

Is the information true for everyone?

If you think the sentence is an OPINION, then:

Write the KEY WORDS, which are clues that tell you how someone thinks, feels, or overstates.

beautiful

Write how the information tells a personal belief or judgment about something.

These sentences describe or overstate the author's feelings.

Is the information true for some people?

yes

68   COPYING IS PROHIBITED   © 2006 Englefield & Associates, Inc.

Note: Student answers may vary. Example responses in italics are for use as a guide.

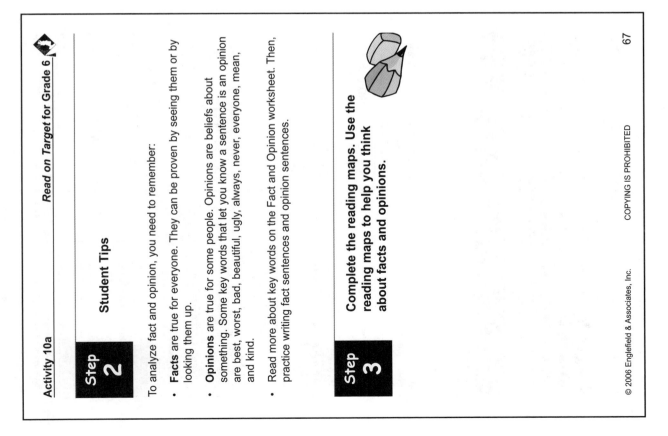

Activity 10a   *Read on Target for Grade 6*

Step 2 — Student Tips

To analyze fact and opinion, you need to remember:

- **Facts** are true for everyone. They can be proven by seeing them or by looking them up.
- **Opinions** are true for some people. Opinions are beliefs about something. Some key words that let you know a sentence is an opinion are best, worst, bad, beautiful, ugly, always, never, everyone, mean, and kind.
- Read more about key words on the Fact and Opinion worksheet. Then, practice writing fact sentences and opinion sentences.

Step 3

Complete the reading maps. Use the reading maps to help you think about facts and opinions.

© 2006 Englefield & Associates, Inc.   COPYING IS PROHIBITED   67

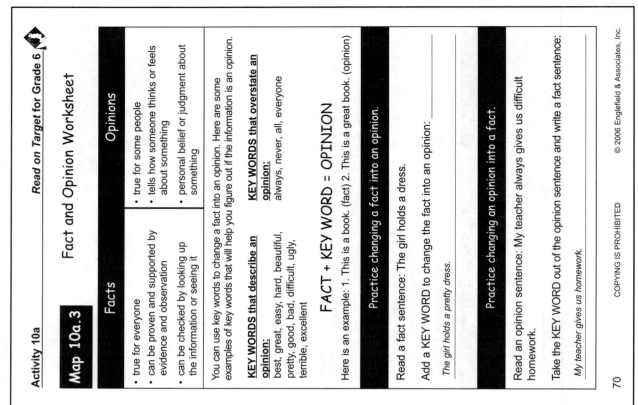

Map 10a.3   Fact and Opinion Worksheet

Facts	Opinions
• true for everyone • can be proven and supported by evidence and observation • can be checked by looking up the information or seeing it	• true for some people • tells how someone thinks or feels about something • personal belief or judgment about something

You can use key words to change a fact into an opinion. Here are some examples of key words that will help you figure out if the information is an opinion.

KEY WORDS that describe an opinion:
best, great, easy, hard, beautiful, pretty, good, bad, difficult, ugly, terrible, excellent

KEY WORDS that overstate an opinion:
always, never, all, everyone

FACT + KEY WORD = OPINION

Here is an example: 1. This is a book. (fact) 2. This is a great book. (opinion)

Practice changing a fact into an opinion.

Read a fact sentence: The girl holds a dress.

Add a KEY WORD to change the fact into an opinion:
The girl holds a pretty dress.

Practice changing an opinion into a fact.

Read an opinion sentence: My teacher always gives us difficult homework.

Take the KEY WORD out of the opinion sentence and write a fact sentence:
My teacher gives us homework.

Note: Student answers may vary. Example responses in italics are for use as a guide.

Map 10a.2   Analyze Aspects of the Text by Examining the Use of Fact and Opinion

I read to figure out if the reading is something that can be proven by evidence or if the reading is a personal belief that tells how someone feels or thinks about something.

Read a sentence from the story.

The city is at least 69 square miles.

If you think the sentence is a FACT, then:

OR

If you think the sentence is an OPINION, then:

Write how the information that you read can be proven by evidence or observation.
It is true for everyone. It can be observed.

Write the KEY WORDS, which are clues that tell you how someone thinks, feels, or overstates.

Write where you would check by looking up the information or where you would see it.
city map; tourism department; encyclopedia

Write how the information tells a personal belief or judgment about something.

Is the information true for everyone?
yes

Is the information true for some people?

Activity 10b

Analyze the Text by Examining the Use of Fact and Opinion

I figure out if the sentence can be proven or is a personal belief that tells how someone feels or thinks.

Step 1   Read the story "My Family Rendezvous."

My Family Rendezvous

I just had the best weekend of my life. My family went to a rendezvous encampment. Everyone at an encampment agrees to dress and to act as if they lived in another time period. Our rendezvous was planned to re-enact life on the Ohio frontier in the 1780s.

Just as people today need clothes to wear, people in the 1700s needed clothing to wear; however, what they wore and how they obtained their clothing back then is very different from today. When I outgrow my clothes, my family shops at a department store. There were no department stores on the Ohio frontier of 1780, so men and women had to make most of their own clothing. Therefore, most of the clothing worn at an encampment is made by hand. The men at the rendezvous wore pants made of animal hides. My stylish pants were made of beautiful deerskin that was the color of wheat and as soft as velvet. My dad paid for the deer hides with a check, and we sewed my pants by hand. It takes much more time to make your clothes by hand than it does to buy them at a store. In 1780, we probably would have had to hunt for the animals instead of buying the

72   COPYING IS PROHIBITED   © 2006 Englefield & Associates, Inc.

Note: Student answers may vary. Example responses in italics are for use as a guide.

Activity 10a

Step 4   **Read the following questions and write your answers.**

1. List two facts from the text.

   Washington, D.C., is the capital of the United States. Washington, D.C., is 69

   square miles in size.

2. What is the author saying about Washington, D.C.?

   The author says Washington, D.C., has many places to visit. This is a fact. The

   author also says everyone would love to visit Washington, D.C. This is an opinion.

3. The author mentioned the garden is beautiful. Is that a fact or an opinion? Explain your answer.

   This is an opinion. The word "beautiful" describes the author's feelings toward the

   garden. This may not be true for all people.

4. Tell why the author says everyone would love to visit Washington, D.C.

   The author enjoyed visiting Washington, D.C., so he assumes everyone will enjoy it.

71

Activity 10b   *Read on Target for Grade 6*

Step 2   **Student Tips**

To analyze fact and opinion, you need to remember:

• **Facts** are true for everyone. They can be proven by seeing them or by looking them up.

• **Opinions** are true for some people. Opinions are beliefs about something. Some key words that let you know a sentence is an opinion are best, worst, bad, beautiful, ugly, always, never, everyone, mean, and kind.

• Read more about key words on the Fact and Opinion worksheet. Then, practice writing fact sentences and opinion sentences.

Step 3   **Complete the reading maps. Use the reading maps to help you think about facts and opinions.**

Activity 10b   *Read on Target for Grade 6*

animal hides. If you weren't a good hunter, it could be a long time before you were able to make new pants or moccasins. Wearing jeans or gym shoes was not permitted at the rendezvous because they were invented after 1800.

Women of that time period wanted to be fashionable, just as all women today buy and wear the current fashions. In colonial days, women wore several long skirts or petticoats that hung to their ankles. Also, it was considered good manners for women and girls to wear some type of head covering all of the time, even to bed! Today some women wear hats for special occasions, but most women do not usually wear hats. Some women today wear T-shirts and shorts or pants, but women in the 1780s were not allowed to wear clothing that showed their elbows or legs. At the encampment, my mother wore a chemise (a long blouse), two brightly colored petticoats, a royal blue vest, and a snow-white hat called a mop cap. The mop cap had two rows of ruffles that framed her face. The ruffles shook like flower petals dancing in the wind when she laughed.

No one laughed during mealtime at the rendezvous. Cooking was serious work. It took a long time to prepare even one meal. Wood had to be chopped for the open fires where we cooked. We all had to be careful that our clothes did not brush against the flames or the coals of the cooking fire. I helped my dad carry water in canvas buckets from a nearby creek to our campsite for meals and safety in case something caught fire. The water was heavy, but since we were camping on a cool day, I hardly missed the running water we have at home. At the encampment, we cooked most of our food on a turning stick called a spit or in heavy black iron pots. There were no refrigerators, microwaves, electric stoves, or paper plates at the rendezvous or in the 1780s, but the food was just as delicious as if we had prepared the food at home.

Activity 10b

Read on Target for Grade 6

Map 10b.2

Analyze Aspects of the Text by Examining the Use of Fact and Opinion

I read to figure out if the reading is something that can be proven by evidence or if the reading is a personal belief that tells how someone feels or thinks about something.

Read a sentence from the story.

Wearing jeans or gym shoes was not permitted at the rendezvous because they were invented after 1800.

If you think the sentence is a FACT, then:

OR

If you think the sentence is an OPINION, then:

Write how the information that you read can be proven by evidence or observation.

You could watch documentaries,

or you could go to a museum.

Write the KEY WORDS, which are clues that tell you how someone thinks, feels, or overstates.

Write where you would check by looking up the information or where you would see it.

You can read about life in the

1780s in an encyclopedia.

Write how the information tells a personal belief or judgment about something.

Is the information true for everyone?

yes

Is the information true for some people?

76

Note: Student answers may vary. Example responses in italics are for use as a guide.

Activity 10b

Read on Target for Grade 6

Map 10b.1

Analyze Aspects of the Text by Examining the Use of Fact and Opinion

I read to figure out if the reading is something that can be proven by evidence or if the reading is a personal belief that tells how someone feels or thinks about something.

Read a sentence from the story.

My stylish pants were made of beautiful deerskin that was a color of wheat and as soft as velvet.

If you think the sentence is a FACT, then:

OR

If you think the sentence is an OPINION, then:

Write how the information that you read can be proven by evidence or observation.

Write the KEY WORDS, which are clues that tell you how someone thinks, feels, or overstates.

stylish, beautiful

Write where you would check by looking up the information or where you would see it.

Write how the information tells a personal belief or judgment about something.

These sentences tell how the

author feels about the clothing.

Is the information true for everyone?

Is the information true for some people?

yes

75

Activity 10b   *Read on Target* for Grade 6

Step 4

Read the following questions and write your answers.

1. List three items from the text that, in your opinion, you would miss if you lived in the 1780s. Explain your opinions.

I would not like it if I couldn't wear gym shoes, jeans, and T-shirts. I can't imagine

not having a refrigerator to keep my food cold. But most of all, I would miss running

water.

2. The author indicated that the rendezvous was the best weekend of his life. Find another opinion statement that describes another enjoyable aspect of the weekend.

The food was just as delicious as if we had prepared the food at home.

My stylish pants were made of beautiful deerskin that was the color of wheat and

as soft as velvet.

3. What facts from the story might make someone choose to go camping at the rendezvous?

The men at the rendezvous wore pants made of animal hides. Our rendezvous

was planned to re-enact life on the Ohio frontier in the 1780s. Wood had to be

chopped for the open fires where we cooked.

4. The author describes a different style of clothing for men and women of the 1780s. Give your opinion about how you would feel wearing similar clothing today.

I would enjoy wearing clothing like the author wore at the rendezvous. The author

describes the clothing as stylish, and the clothing also sounds comfortable. I like

clothes that are stylish and comfortable.

78   COPYING IS PROHIBITED   © 2006 Englefield & Associates, Inc.

Note: Student answers may vary. Example responses in italics are for use as a guide.

Activity 10b   *Read on Target* for Grade 6

Map 10b.3   Fact and Opinion Worksheet

Facts	Opinions
• true for everyone • can be proven and supported by evidence and observation • can be checked by looking up the information or seeing it	• true for some people • tells how someone thinks or feels about something • personal belief or judgment about something

You can use key words to change a fact into an opinion. Here are some examples of key words that will help you figure out if the information is an opinion.

KEY WORDS that describe an opinion:
best, great, easy, hard, beautiful, pretty, good, bad, difficult, ugly, terrible, excellent

KEY WORDS that overstate an opinion:
always, never, all, everyone

FACT + KEY WORD = OPINION

Here is an example: 1. This is a book. (fact) 2. This is a great book. (opinion)

Practice changing a fact into an opinion.

Read a fact sentence: I have a puppy.

Add a KEY WORD to change the fact into an opinion:

I have a beautiful puppy.

Practice changing an opinion into a fact.

Read an opinion sentence: Students always go to the football games.

Take the KEY WORD out of the opinion sentence and write a fact sentence:

Students go to the football games.

© 2006 Englefield & Associates, Inc.   COPYING IS PROHIBITED   77

Troubleshooting: Understanding Fact and Opinion

Determining fact and opinion is an important skill because not only is it assessed in both fiction and nonfiction, it is also a building block for understanding other skills, such as propaganda. Students may not always have the knowledge base to feel secure that they can identify fact from fiction, but they need to know that a fact can be proven to be true or not true, even if they do not know the answer. An opinion varies because it is subjective, even if most people hold the same opinion.

Example:

   Fact: A genius is a person with an IQ of over 140. Sarah is a genius.

   Opinion: My friend is a genius when it comes to music.

In the example above, genius is used in two different ways. In the first sentence, even if you are not sure the true definition of a genius is correct, it can be proven. In the second sentence, it is an exaggeration to say how great the friend is; therefore, it is only an opinion.

Example:

   Fact: Ted thinks his mother is beautiful.

   Opinion: Ted's mother is beautiful.

Nitpicking? Possibly, but the statement is a fact because the information is what Ted thinks. The statement can be proven by asking Ted what he thinks. The statement can also be determined to be true for everyone who asked Ted what he thinks. It can be proven by observation and checked. Students can become confused because a KEY WORD is in the statement. Teach your students to consider what the statement is saying. When the statement is changed to say simply, "Ted's mother is beautiful," it becomes an opinion. Students need to build a clear vocabulary base in understanding words that are subjective. It isn't difficult to do and can be incorporated into a journal with reasons why words are subjective.

11

Explain How and Why an Author Uses Contents of a Text to Support His/Her Purpose for Writing

---

Teaching Tips

What Do Students Need to Know?

Students need to determine the reason for the author's purpose for writing. The author writes according to the purpose of the story. The reason the story was written has a direct effect on the content and vocabulary of the story. For example, if the purpose is to provide information, facts and data will be in the story. If the purpose of the story is for enjoyment, the information will contain expressive words and descriptions that the reader will enjoy. Students also need to know the vocabulary that is embedded in the word **"explain."** When the word "explain" is used in a question, students need to answer **"why"** (reason) and **"how"** (process). "Why" is similar to answering a persuasion question and "how" is similar to telling directions. When teachers focus instruction on the embedded vocabulary of "explain," a clear understanding of the requirements and expectations of the task occurs.

Use of the Reading Map

When students understand the purpose for reading, they gain direction and are aware of the reason the story was written. Before the students begin reading, they need to have the purpose for reading in mind. By answering a question, which includes the word "explain," students are asked to tell why or how.

The reading map will guide students to:

- Read the definitions of the purposes for fiction, poetry, and nonfiction.

- Circle the type of writing in the box on the left (fiction, poetry, nonfiction).

- Write the author's purpose in the box (why the story was written).

- Write a sentence or sentences from the story that shows an example of the author's purpose (how the author tells the purpose for the writing).

rules, each state acted like its own unique government—almost like an independent country. Each state could run its government just the way it wanted to."

Carlos replied, "To make matters worse, some people started thinking about revolting in order to solve their problems. The new government really needed something in writing!"

The boys' teacher, Mrs. Thompson, heard Juan and Carlos' discussion and stopped by their table. Mrs. Thompson explained to them that there are also specific powers defined in the Constitution. Some of the federal powers included the right to collect taxes, to declare war, and to regulate trade. Other powers were left to the states and reserved for the people.

"In my opinion," Mrs. Thompson said, "one very important power reserved for the people is the right to own property." She also told them, "Although many powers are defined as separate, you will see that in some cases, the federal government and the states have the ability to act at both federal and state levels."

Mrs. Thompson then explained, "The Constitution has a preamble, seven articles, and twenty-seven amendments. It basically sets up a system that divides powers between the federal (central government) and the states. It also established a balance by setting up three branches of government: the executive branch, the legislative branch, and the judicial branch. The executive branch enforces the laws; the legislative branch makes the laws; the judicial branch interprets the laws. Thus, we have three separate branches that can check and balance one another. This is known as the separation of powers."

"I get it!" Juan exclaimed. "That really makes sense! No one part of the government can ever become too powerful. I think everyone should know why the constitution was written. Without it, we would not have the type of government, rules, freedoms, and rights we have today. The Constitution is a really important document."

Activity 11a

Explain How and Why an Author Uses Contents of a Text to Support His/Her Purpose for Writing

I tell the process (how) and the reason (why) the story was written.

Step 1   Read the selection "The Constitution."

The Constitution

During a class trip to the library, Carlos and Juan were assigned a project to read and study information about the Constitution of the United States. They learned that the Constitution is our nation's basis for laws. They read that it established not only a group of independent states but a central form of government as well. It defined the powers of our government and established the protection of rights of all states and every person.

Juan and Carlos found out that after the Revolutionary War, our government was made up of an association of states. First, The Articles of Confederation were written. In it, our founding fathers established a national government, but they gave independence to each state and did not require states to work together to solve national problems. Carlos learned that the Constitution was written to develop a central government with three separate branches. Rules for trade between states and countries, as well as tax issues, were defined.

Juan said, "It was a good idea to write down something that tells what the responsibilities of our government are. I didn't realize how important it is to have a guide of basic laws that apply to all of the states."

Carlos said, "Those 13 states must have been a weak association back then, without any central government to hold them together."

"You know what?" said Juan, "I read that without the Constitution, there would be problems with providing money to support the government. Can you imagine a government being totally dependent on the states for money to operate? Without the permission of the states, the new government could not enforce laws, tax the states, or tax the people. Without a clear set of written

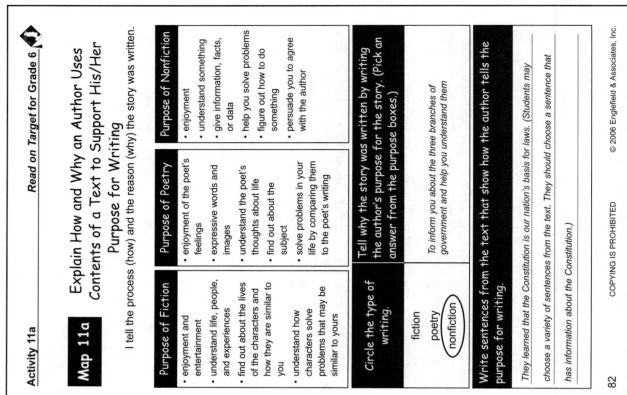

Activity 11a   *Read on Target* for Grade 6

Map 11a — Explain How and Why an Author Uses Contents of a Text to Support His/Her Purpose for Writing

I tell the process (how) and the reason (why) the story was written.

Purpose of Fiction	Purpose of Poetry	Purpose of Nonfiction
• enjoyment and entertainment • understand life, people, and experiences • find out about the lives of the characters and how they are similar to you • understand how characters solve problems that may be similar to yours	• enjoyment of the poet's feelings • expressive words and images • understand the poet's thoughts about life • find out about the subject • solve problems in your life by comparing them to the poet's writing	• enjoyment • understand something • give information, facts, or data • help you solve problems • figure out how to do something • persuade you to agree with the author

Tell why the story was written by writing the author's purpose for the story. (Pick an answer from the purpose boxes.)

To inform you about the three branches of government and help you understand them

Circle the type of writing.

fiction
poetry
(nonfiction)

Write sentences from the text that show how the author tells the purpose for writing.

They learned that the Constitution is our nation's basis for laws. (Students may choose a variety of sentences from the text. They should choose a sentence that has information about the Constitution.)

82   COPYING IS PROHIBITED   © 2006 Englefield & Associates, Inc.

Note: Student answers may vary. Example responses in italics are for use as a guide.

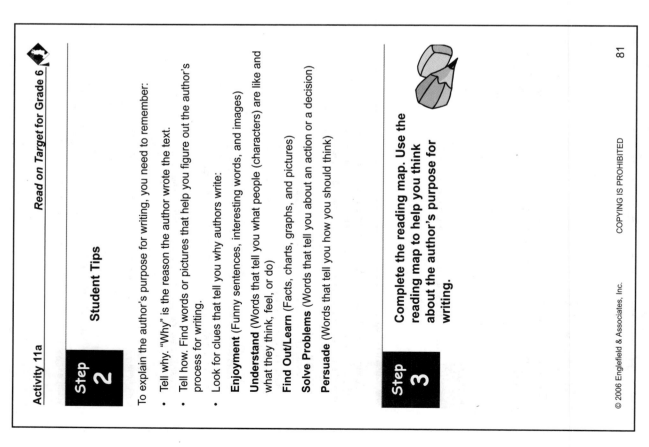

Activity 11a   *Read on Target* for Grade 6

Step 2 — Student Tips

To explain the author's purpose for writing, you need to remember:

- Tell why. "Why" is the reason the author wrote the text.
- Tell how. Find words or pictures that help you figure out the author's process for writing.
- Look for clues that tell you why authors write:

Enjoyment (Funny sentences, interesting words, and images)

Understand (Words that tell you what people (characters) are like and what they think, feel, or do)

Find Out/Learn (Facts, charts, graphs, and pictures)

Solve Problems (Words that tell you about an action or a decision)

Persuade (Words that tell you how you should think)

Step 3

Complete the reading map. Use the reading map to help you think about the author's purpose for writing.

81   © 2006 Englefield & Associates, Inc.   COPYING IS PROHIBITED

Activity 11b

Explain How and Why an Author Uses Contents of a Text to Support His/Her Purpose for Writing

I tell the process (how) and the reason (why) the story was written.

Step 1 Read the announcement "Drama Club Meeting."

Drama Club Meeting

Attention All Meridian Middle School Students

A membership meeting for the Meridian Middle School Drama Club will be held Monday, September 19, in the media center from 3:00 p.m. to 4:00 p.m. Come meet current members of our club to find out how much fun it is to be a thespian. The Drama Club is open to all middle school students.

We need all kinds of people to be in Drama Club.

- People with desire to be on stage such as actors, comics, singers, and dancers—we need you. Come and entertain your peers.
- People who like to work off stage—we need you. We can teach you how to be a prop manager, a screen technician, a lighting technician, and a sound technician.
- People who are creative and artistic—we need you. Backdrop artists, costume designers, and cover designers are needed.
- People who like to work with computers—we need you. Help print our programs or control the special effects graphics.
- There is a place for everyone who wants to join Drama Club.

This year's production is "Middle School Madness."

We meet Monday and Thursday of every week from 3:00 p.m. to 4:00 p.m.

Sign up on the bulletin board in the cafeteria, and show up in the media center on Monday. You should come because you will have fun. Free refreshments will be served. See you there!

84   COPYING IS PROHIBITED   © 2006 Englefield & Associates, Inc.

Note: Student answers may vary. Example responses in italics are for use as a guide.

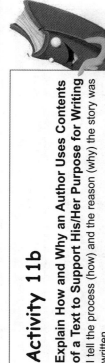

Step 4 Read the following questions and write your answers.

1. What is the author's purpose for writing this sentence: "The Constitution has a preamble, seven articles, and twenty-seven amendments. It basically sets up a system that divides powers between the federal (central government) and the states"?

   The author's purpose is to inform people about the three branches of government.

2. What is the author's purpose for writing this sentence: " Mrs. Thompson explained to them that there are also specific powers defined in the Constitution"?

   The author's purpose is to help the reader understand what the Constitution does.

3. What type of writing is this text?

   It is nonfiction.

4. Write a sentence from the text that has factual information that helps the reader understand the author's purpose.

   Student answers will vary. Responses should provide a sentence that includes

   factual information about the three branches of government and helps students

   understand the government's structure and purpose.

© 2006 Englefield & Associates, Inc.   COPYING IS PROHIBITED   83

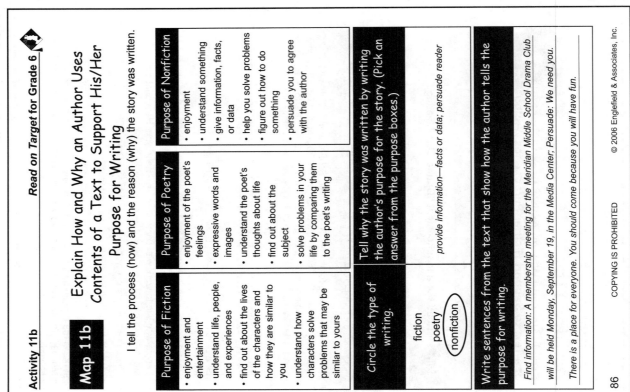

Activity 11b   *Read on Target* for Grade 6

Map 11b — Explain How and Why an Author Uses Contents of a Text to Support His/Her Purpose for Writing

I tell the process (how) and the reason (why) the story was written.

Purpose of Fiction	Purpose of Poetry	Purpose of Nonfiction
• enjoyment and entertainment • understand life, people, and experiences • find out about the lives of the characters and how they are similar to you • understand how characters solve problems that may be similar to yours	• enjoyment of the poet's feelings • expressive words and images • understand the poet's thoughts about life • find out about the subject • solve problems in your life by comparing them to the poet's writing	• enjoyment • understand something • give information, facts, or data • help you solve problems • figure out how to do something • persuade you to agree with the author

Circle the type of writing.

fiction
poetry
(nonfiction)

Tell why the story was written by writing the author's purpose for the story. (Pick an answer from the purpose boxes.)

provide information—facts or data; persuade reader

Write sentences from the text that show how the author tells the purpose for writing.

Find information: A membership meeting for the Meridian Middle School Drama Club will be held Monday, September 19, in the Media Center; Persuade: We need you. There is a place for everyone. You should come because you will have fun.

86   COPYING IS PROHIBITED   © 2006 Englefield & Associates, Inc.

Note: Student answers may vary. Example responses in italics are for use as a guide.

Activity 11b   *Read on Target* for Grade 6

Step 2 — Student Tips

To explain the author's purpose for writing, you need to remember:

- Tell why. "Why" is the reason the author wrote the text.
- Tell how. Find words or pictures that help you figure out the author's process for writing.
- Look for clues that tell you why authors write:

Enjoyment (Funny sentences, interesting words, and images)

Understand (Words that tell you what people (characters) are like and what they think, feel, or do)

Find Out/Learn (Facts, charts, graphs, and pictures)

Solve Problems (Words that tell you about an action or a decision)

Persuade (Words that tell you how you should think)

Step 3 — Complete the reading map. Use the reading map to help you think about the author's purpose for writing.

© 2006 Englefield & Associates, Inc.   COPYING IS PROHIBITED   85

Note: Student answers may vary. Example responses in italics are for use as a guide.

Read on Target **for Grade 6**

Activity 11b

Step 4

Read the following questions and write your answers.

1. How did you determine the author's purpose for writing the announcement?

   The announcement included information, facts, and some persuasive words.

2. How did the author try to persuade you to attend the meeting?

   The author gave reasons why all types of people are needed in the Drama Club.

   The author also said free refreshments will be served and all who attend will have

   fun.

3. If the author's purpose was changed to **enjoyment**, how would the announcement be different?

   Student answers will vary. Some suggested responses include: The announcement

   might include a funny story or a riddle. The words in the announcement might not

   be persuasive or informative.

4. Do you think the announcement is successful in achieving its purpose? Why or why not?

   Student answers may vary. Yes, the announcement was successful. It convinced

   me that I am needed. I believe there is a place for me in the Drama Club, and I

   know where and when the meeting will be held.

© 2006 Englefield & Associates, Inc.   COPYING IS PROHIBITED   87

Troubleshooting: How to Use Text to Explain the Author's Purpose

Before a student can understand an author's purpose for a piece of writing, it is helpful for him or her to understand certain genres are more likely to be written for certain purposes. There are four basic purposes for which an author creates a work: to entertain, to express opinions, to inform, or to persuade.

For fiction, the most common purpose is to entertain. However, under that general purpose, part of the entertaining process may be enjoyment, understanding different ideas and cultures, finding out about different people and their lives, or solving problems that are interesting to the reader. Poetry may fall under the entertainment purpose; this could be enjoyment of the beauty of the words and images or enjoyment of reading the poet's feelings. Another purpose of poetry is to understand ideas the poet presents about life. Other purposes would be to find out about the subject discussed or to solve problems by comparing the poet's writing to situations in your own life. Purposes of nonfiction can be enjoyment, but more often they are to understand about something, to find information, to solve problems, to figure out how to do something, or to persuade the reader to agree with the author.

Understanding the author's purpose is a key element and a stepping stone to other tested concepts, such as understanding an author's tone and opinion. It also helps students to analyze whether or not they feel the author's opinion is valid. This is a critical skill for understanding the concept of propaganda and its effects on the reader. Certainly, as readers of common propaganda, we all want to be educated and critical evaluators of the validity of the propaganda we are bombarded with every day.

The process by which we can determine the author's purpose is a simple one; first, we must consider what type of writing the selection is; next, we ask ourselves why is the author writing this selection; and the important step we cannot leave out, but often do, is to support our decision with proof from the selection. We do this by looking for specific details that would give us our answers.

If the piece is nonfiction, we look for clues such as facts, details, opinion statements, charts, and other data formats to determine the author's purpose. Obviously, an abundance of facts and details would indicate that the author's purpose is to inform. Charts and graphs would possibly indicate solving problems, as well as giving information. Opinions would indicate the author's intent to persuade or to express opinions to the reader. The consistency of the type of clues would be what the reader hones in on to determine the author's purpose.

Similarly, in fiction and poetry, it is more common to see interesting words and images, entertaining topics, and suspense techniques that lead to the enjoyment of the piece. As the teacher, guide the students in their reading to notice these clues the author gives.

When using the reading map, the students will need a lot of guidance to determine the author's purpose, but your most important role will be to model the behavior of an active reader in helping them discover clues from the text that will support their analyses of the author's purpose.

12 Evaluate and Critique the Text for Organizational Structure

---

Teaching Tips

What Do Students Need to Know?

When students evaluate and critique the text for organizational structure, they need to determine if the reading flows from idea to idea and why it is a strength or a weakness. Students state opinions of how effective the organization is and may give reasons why they believe the organization is more effective or less effective.

Use of the Reading Map

When students evaluate and critique the text for organizational structure, they determine what form of organization the author chose. Next, they determine whether the form of organization made the story more effective or less effective and give reasons why.

The reading map will guide students to:

- Read the definitions of the types of organizational structure.

- Determine the type of organization used by the author.

- List some ways the organization is a strength or a weakness (more effective or less effective).

- Explain how effective the organization of the nonfiction writing is.

- Determine whether the text flows from idea to idea.

- Explain why the organization is effective or not effective.

Step 2　Student Tips

To help you understand whether the text flows from idea to idea and why the organizational structure of the text is a strength or a weakness, you need to remember:

- There are four basic ways an author organizes the writing.

  Time order (chronological)

  Cause and effect order (links what happened and why it happened)

  Order of importance (information given in the text is ordered from least important to most important or vice versa)

  Compare and contrast order (looks at how information is alike or different from other information)

- To think about whether the way the information is presented is clear or confusing

- To consider whether the author's organization kept you interested in or excited about the information or whether it made the information seem boring

- To see if you were able to follow the sequence of information or if it was difficult for you to follow

- There can be more than one type of order within a single text

Step 3

Complete the reading map. Use the reading map to help you think about evaluating and critiquing the text for organizational structure.

Activity 12a

Evaluate and Critique the Text for Organizational Structure

I discuss whether the reading flows from idea to idea and why the organization is a strength or a weakness.

Step 1　Read the poem "Happy Birthday, U.S.A."

Happy Birthday, U.S.A.

July 4th, 1776—In Philadelphia, a day to rejoice,
　Our founding fathers raised a voice.
　The Declaration of Independence,
　Signed by one and all from this day hence.

　　　Bands played,
Contests, games, and food were made.
People laughed, danced, and sang,
While all the bells of freedom rang.

Today—The tradition continues from year to year,
As we remember what we all hold dear.
Our democracy, freedom, rights, laws
　Are remembered by one and all.

Our parades, picnics, and fireworks are a clue,
And symbolize our freedom—red, white, and blue.
Yes, parties, fun, and festivities are a way,
　To celebrate this special day.

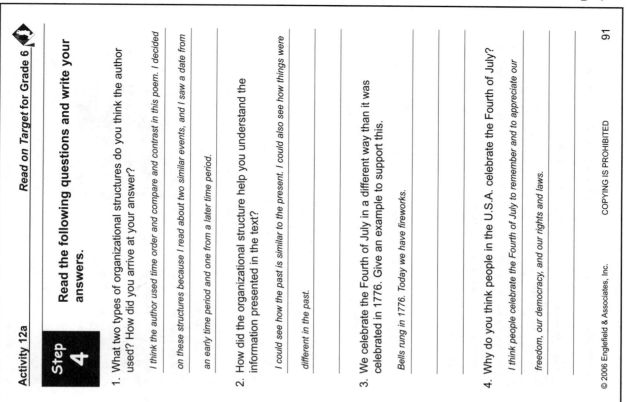

Activity 12a

Step 4

Read the following questions and write your answers.

1. What two types of organizational structures do you think the author used? How did you arrive at your answer?

   I think the author used time order and compare and contrast in this poem. I decided on these structures because I read about two similar events, and I saw a date from an early time period and one from a later time period.

2. How did the organizational structure help you understand the information presented in the text?

   I could see how the past is similar to the present. I could also see how things were different in the past.

3. We celebrate the Fourth of July in a different way than it was celebrated in 1776. Give an example to support this.

   Bells rung in 1776. Today we have fireworks.

4. Why do you think people in the U.S.A. celebrate the Fourth of July?

   I think people celebrate the Fourth of July to remember and to appreciate our freedom, our democracy, and our rights and laws.

© 2006 Englefield & Associates, Inc.   COPYING IS PROHIBITED   91

Note: Student answers may vary. Example responses in italics are for use as a guide.

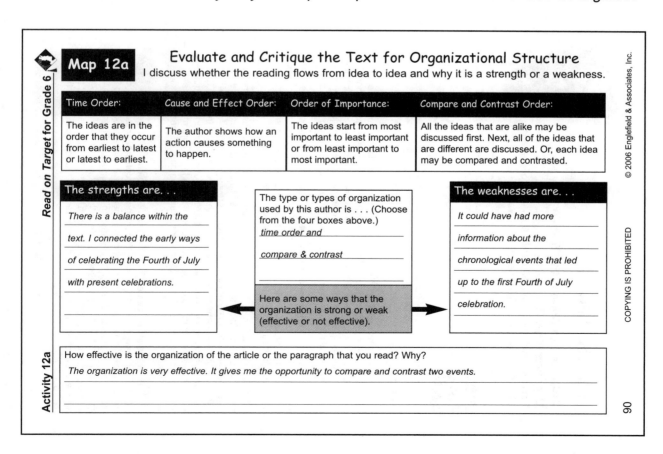

Map 12a   ## Evaluate and Critique the Text for Organizational Structure
I discuss whether the reading flows from idea to idea and why it is a strength or a weakness.

© 2006 Englefield & Associates, Inc.

Time Order:	Cause and Effect Order:	Order of Importance:	Compare and Contrast Order:
The ideas are in the order that they occur from earliest to latest or latest to earliest.	The author shows how an action causes something to happen.	The ideas start from most important to least important or from least important to most important.	All the ideas that are alike may be discussed first. Next, all of the ideas that are different are discussed. Or, each idea may be compared and contrasted.

The strengths are. . .

There is a balance within the text. I connected the early ways of celebrating the Fourth of July with present celebrations.

The type or types of organization used by this author is . . . (Choose from the four boxes above.)
time order and

compare & contrast

Here are some ways that the organization is strong or weak (effective or not effective).

The weaknesses are. . .

It could have had more information about the chronological events that led up to the first Fourth of July celebration.

COPYING IS PROHIBITED

Activity 12a

How effective is the organization of the article or the paragraph that you read? Why?
The organization is very effective. It gives me the opportunity to compare and contrast two events.

90

Activity 12b

Evaluate and Critique the Text for Organizational Structure

I discuss whether the reading flows from idea to idea and why the organization is a strength or a weakness.

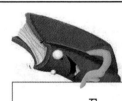

Step 1 Read the story "Cliff Jumping."

Cliff Jumping

For as long as I could remember, I had heard my dad's and my uncle's stories about jumping off the cliffs into a lake in Canada. I never really thought much about it except that they must have been crazy or exaggerating, or both. They used to brag about climbing cliffs that were 30 feet tall and jumping into the water below that was over 80 feet deep. Who would do anything so silly?

One year, we went on vacation to that very same lake, Lake Manitou. When my dad first launched our boat, I said jokingly, "Hey, Dad, how about taking us to the cliffs?" I expected him to take us to a big rock on shore and say something like, "Well, it used to seem much bigger when we were kids."

As we sped along over the clear blue water, the shore began to change from low, rocky outcroppings, to ledges that became higher and higher. They were pine-covered, with some of the pines actually growing out of the faces of the cliffs. Sometimes, there would be tall ledges that jutted out over the lake, but there were rocks in the water below, as if there had once been an earthquake that had shaken them loose from their rocky homes. I was sure my dad and uncle had been telling tales as tall as those cliffs. Jumping off those cliffs looked dangerous.

Then we rounded the next bluff; we saw boats anchored in the water just off shore. Dad slowed the boat and cut the engine. We could hear laughter and shouts of excitement and encouragement. There, cut into the rock shore by Mother Nature herself, was a perfectly smooth right angle cliff that rose into the air about 30 feet. The water lapped gently at the high smooth wall. The water was a deep, deep green that seemed to hint at the depth below. My dad threw out the 100-foot anchor line, and it disappeared right up to where it was tied to the boat.

Activity 12b

Kids and adults were climbing up a steep rock face a short way down the shore. They were holding a rope tied to some trees; it helped them scale the rocks. Some people were perched on a lower ledge that jutted out of the smooth face of the cliff like a balcony on a house, while some scrambled all the way to the top. As I watched, you could see every single climber pause as he or she looked from the top of the cliff into the water below. Some people jumped quickly as if they just wanted to get it over with. Their screams of excitement rang out as they plunged into the water. The scene made me want to try it and to run away at the same time. Others stayed at the top for what seemed like forever. You could tell they wanted to jump but just couldn't. I understood exactly how they felt.

Did I dare try it? Dad seemed to understand. He said, "Come on, Lauren, I will, if you will." As if something were drawing me to insanity, I jumped over the side of the boat into the water and swam to shore. I dragged myself up those rocky cliffs holding onto the rope as if it was my link to heaven. Did I mention that I am afraid of heights? As I climbed out on the ledge, I held onto a nearby pine tree. I looked over the edge to see the same frightening sight all those others had seen. What was I doing up on this ledge? Such things are for adventure seekers only.

Suddenly from behind, Dad took my hand and said, "Come on, Lauren, you'll love it." I ignored the voice in my head that kept telling me I was too scared to jump. "On the count of three," Dad said enthusiastically. I held my breath and jumped. It seemed as if I would never reach the water. The air rushed by me as my heart seemed to pound through my chest. Then whoosh, into the cold depths, we kept going down, down, down. I began to wonder if I had enough air to get back up to the surface. As my head broke back into the sunlight, I gasped. I did it! I was in one piece, alive, and I had jumped. My dad was laughing and gasping for air just like I was.

I wonder what my children will think someday about my story of jumping off a cliff. I know one thing for sure—there will only be one story, because I won't be doing it again.

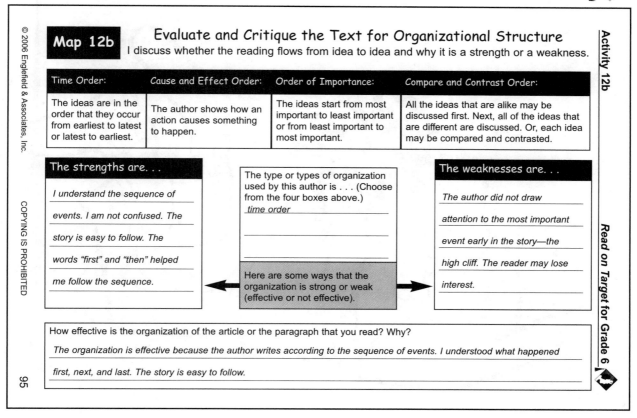

Note: Student answers may vary. Example responses in italics are for use as a guide.

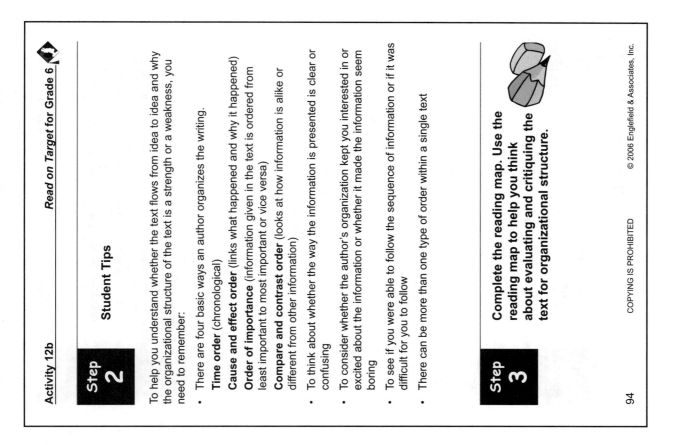

Note: Student answers may vary. Example responses in italics are for use as a guide.

Step 4

Read the following questions and write your answers.

1. What type of organizational structure did the author use?

   The author used time order for the organizational structure.

2. What words in the text gave you information as to how the author organized the information?

   For as long as I could remember...

   One year...

   When my dad first launched... Then we...

3. What details did the author include to help make this story seem organized?

   When my dad first launched our boat... As we sped along over the clear blue water.

   Then, we rounded the next bluff. As I climbed out on the ledge...

4. How else could the author have ended the story?

   The author might not have jumped. The author could have started the story by

   talking about being at the top of the cliff. The author could have ended the story by

   describing a lesson learned: overcoming something scary can build courage.

96   COPYING IS PROHIBITED   © 2006 Englefield & Associates, Inc.

Troubleshooting: Evaluating and Critiquing the Text for Organizational Structure

Students don't give much thought to the organization of their own writing, and they give even less when evaluating another writer's work. Consequently, students need reminders that nonfiction must have a clear order to be effective. **Time order** (chronological) is perhaps the simplest to understand. It is easy to identify when the author has made an error in the chain of events. Students should look for a clear presentation of the events from the beginning to the end. Words that will clue students include first, next, finally, etc. Biographies are a good example of text where time order is effective.

If a student is reading a nonfiction piece using **cause and effect order**, it becomes very complex because there are several logical ways to organize cause and effect. Cause and effect order links what happens to why something happens, and it is rarely a simple "because of this, that" situation. There are usually multiple parts to cause and effect relationships. Students need to see this because if we, as teachers, say there is only one way to write cause and effect, we are going to impair students' abilities to see logic.

For example, an author might choose to start with the causes of the Civil War and work into the effect. Another author might choose to show how a chain of cause and effect incidents led to the rise of literacy in the Middle Ages. Another author could choose to begin with the effect and work back through the causes. In any case, **your explanation will be much stronger with reading maps that help students visualize your lesson**. There can be multiple causes and effects, and the order can vary. Teachers may need to use the cause and effect reading maps to provide additional direction for students in conjunction with the Evaluate and Critique for Organizational Structure reading map.

Here are some examples of how cause and effect can vary.

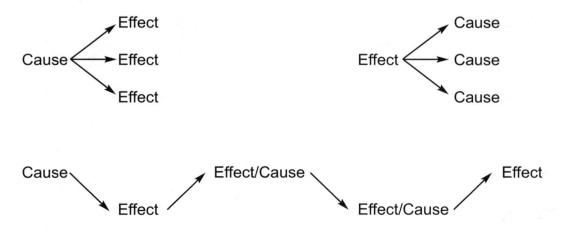

The most important element for students to see when evaluating cause and effect order is that the author has clearly stated the cause and effect relationship regardless of the path he or she takes. There should be clear connections between cause and effect with the use of clue words that show cause and effect (because, therefore, as a result, etc). There is a logical order apparent, and there are ample facts or details to support the cause and effect relationship.

Order of importance is not nearly so complex. The student simply needs to look at the reasons given and analyze if the order goes from least important to most important or vice versa. The logic for this order is that the writer is building suspense to keep the reader's interest. If a trivial detail is given toward the end, it minimizes the importance of the point being made. This is an excellent organizational technique for persuasive papers. The student should look for words that show the level of importance, such as first, second, mainly, most important, etc.

Compare and contrast order often falls short when students are using this type of organization for the simple reason that they don't always see the balance and the completion necessary to do this kind of writing. The author must clearly identify the two subjects that are being compared. Specific details of similarity or difference must be balanced. The writing should be easy to follow. For example, the author might use one of the orders shown below.

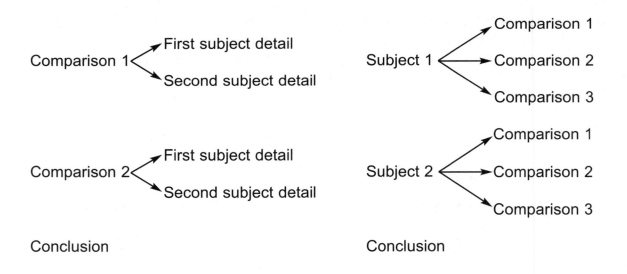

There should be clue words that clearly show similarities and differences, such as like, similar to, unlike, etc. There should be a conclusion that summarizes how the subjects are alike or different.

Although complex, students can usually identify the effectiveness of the text in these areas. The difficulty lies in verbalizing the reasons the organization is effective or is ineffective.

13 Evaluate and Critique the Text for Logic and Reasoning

Teaching Tips

What Do Students Need to Know?

To evaluate and critique logic and reasoning, students need to determine if the author's writing appeals to facts, reasons, and evidence, or if it appeals to feelings, emotions, and opinions. Students will need to understand that logical strengths are facts, reasons, or evidence. When the information is only backed up by feelings, emotions, and opinions, it is a weak argument. Students need to determine if there is enough evidence or too little evidence to support what the author wants the reader to believe. The student will tell if the information is biased and if there are enough facts, reasons, and evidence to support the author's belief.

Use of the Reading Map

When students evaluate and critique the text for logic and reasoning, they determine if the reading relies more on facts or emotions/feelings.

The reading map will guide students to:

- Write the author's belief.

- List the sentences from the text that contain facts, reasons, or evidence.

- List the sentences from the text that contain feelings, emotions, or opinions.

- Tell if the information relies more on facts or feelings.

- Determine if the information is biased (slanted to convince the reader to believe the author's opinion).

- Determine if the information has enough evidence to support the author's belief.

Activity 13a

Evaluate and Critique the Text for Logic and Reasoning

I tell if the reading is backed up by reasons and evidence.

Step 1

Read the article "Help Scientists Study the Ecosystem."

Help Scientists Study the Ecosystem

Some scientists study the ecosystem. An ecosystem includes groups of living and non-living things that interact with one another. Scientists know that ecosystems can vary in size. They can be as small as a puddle or as large as the planet Earth. Temperature, light, food, and population density are some of the factors that make up an ecosystem.

Ongoing studies focus on how changing one or more of the ecosystem factors impacts the entire ecosystem. For example, a fire in Yellowstone National Park completely changed the nature of the system. There are no longer large trees, moss, or large bushes. After a short time, small grass, shrubs, and flowers grew. The small vulnerable animals had to move to a different place to survive. The loss of so much beauty and wildlife saddened the whole country.

It is the opinion of many people that fires can be devastating. Many scientists think there should be a quicker response time to put out forest fires. They also think more money needs to be spent on protecting the environment. After seeing displaced animals, many people in the community feel the same way. Lobbying efforts are in place to provide additional money for studying the ecosystem.

Scientists will continue to study the impact of natural events on the environment. Their work is a valuable asset to all; however, money is desperately needed to continue to study ecosystems. If you would like to contribute financial support, please send your check or money order to a local organization. You never know what plants or animals you might be saving.

Step 2

Student Tips

To help you evaluate and critique the text for logic and reasoning, you need to remember:

- Logic and reasoning skills are similar to determining fact and opinion.
- Use the left side of the reading map to list the information that is backed up with facts, reasons, or evidence.
- Use the right side of the reading map to list the information that includes feelings, emotions, or opinions.
- **Completing the chart in the reading map will show you the balance of the argument.**
- This reading map helps you recognize persuasive text and helps you to not be influenced by persuasive feelings. It also helps you recognize texts that are more factual and are backed by reasons and evidence.

Step 3

Complete the reading map. Use the reading map to help you think about evaluating and critiquing for logic and reasoning.

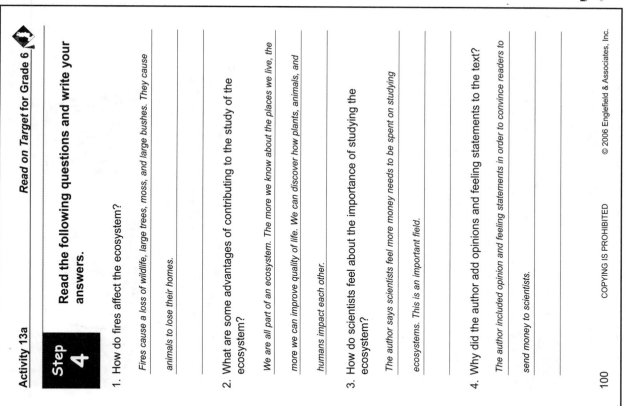

Activity 13a

Step 4

Read the following questions and write your answers.

1. How do fires affect the ecosystem?

   Fires cause a loss of wildlife, large trees, moss, and large bushes. They cause

   animals to lose their homes.

2. What are some advantages of contributing to the study of the ecosystem?

   We are all part of an ecosystem. The more we know about the places we live, the

   more we can discover how plants, animals, and

   humans impact each other.

3. How do scientists feel about the importance of studying the ecosystem?

   The author says scientists feel more money needs to be spent on studying

   ecosystems. This is an important field.

4. Why did the author add opinions and feeling statements to the text?

   The author included opinion and feeling statements in order to convince readers to

   send money to scientists.

100   © 2006 Englefield & Associates, Inc.

COPYING IS PROHIBITED

Note: Student answers may vary. Example responses in italics are for use as a guide.

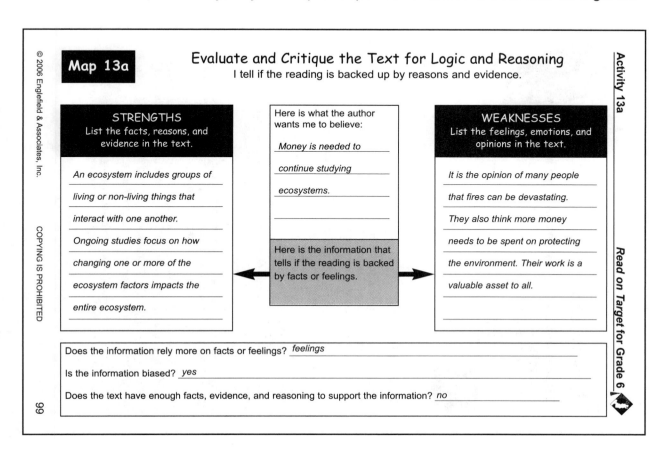

Map 13a

Evaluate and Critique the Text for Logic and Reasoning
I tell if the reading is backed up by reasons and evidence.

STRENGTHS
List the facts, reasons, and evidence in the text.

An ecosystem includes groups of

living or non-living things that

interact with one another.

Ongoing studies focus on how

changing one or more of the

ecosystem factors impacts the

entire ecosystem.

Here is what the author wants me to believe:

Money is needed to

continue studying

ecosystems.

Here is the information that tells if the reading is backed by facts or feelings.

WEAKNESSES
List the feelings, emotions, and opinions in the text.

It is the opinion of many people

that fires can be devastating.

They also think more money

needs to be spent on protecting

the environment. Their work is a

valuable asset to all.

Does the information rely more on facts or feelings? *feelings*

Is the information biased? *yes*

Does the text have enough facts, evidence, and reasoning to support the information? *no*

Activity 13a

Read on Target for Grade 6

© 2006 Englefield & Associates, Inc.

COPYING IS PROHIBITED

99

Activity 13b

Evaluate and Critique the Text for Logic and Reasoning

I tell if the reading is backed up by reasons and evidence.

Step 1 Read the story "Who is Right?"

Who Is Right?

Joelle's brother Mark was just about to turn sixteen. One day he came home from school extremely upset. He had just heard that the state legislature was going to raise the driving age to eighteen.

"That is just totally stupid," complained Mark. "Just when I get to drive, those adults in the legislature want to ruin it for me!"

Joelle was only twelve, but she understood how much Mark was looking forward to getting his license. She was hoping he could take her friends and her around to all the places they wanted to go. Mark had told her he would drive her places when he got his license. All she had to do was wash the car for him once a month. It seemed like a reasonable trade-off to Joelle. A car wash was definitely worth having rides to the mall and to the movies.

Joelle heard her mother explaining insurance statistics to Mark. The legislators had been using this information to support their new bill. She said almost 75 percent of sixteen-year-old drivers have an accident.

Mark retorted, "Maybe 75 percent of eighteen-year-old drivers would have accidents, too, because it's inexperience, not age, that makes the difference."

Joelle thought about that and decided it made sense. In fact, it was the first thing that Mark had said that afternoon that really made sense to her.

Joelle's mother continued, "Legislators feel sixteen-year-old kids are just too reckless. They don't think about the consequences of their actions. And I have to agree with them."

Activity 13b

Mark answered, "Mom, how can you generalize like that? You're stereotyping people. Maybe some sixteen year olds are like that, but so are some eighteen year olds. Believe it or not, there are also some really responsible sixteen year olds. Think about this: how am I going to get a job if I don't have a way to get there? I can't save money for college if I don't have a job. For every reason those legislators give for not permitting sixteen year olds to drive, I bet I have a reason they should."

His mother looked at him thoughtfully, but she didn't say anything. Mark continued, "I also wanted to join the Big Brother program. I thought I would make a great mentor. But I can't do anything like that if I don't have a way to get there. Besides, Dad says we need to watch our money, and I could be a big help if I had my license and could get a job."

"I don't suppose the legislators thought about that, but more about safety issues," answered his mother. "Maybe I'll call our congressman's office and give him my opinions."

"You know, Mom, I think I will, too," declared Mark.

Joelle just looked at them, thinking about all they had said. Then she thought, "I sure hope I can drive when I am sixteen. Maybe I'll call the congressman's office, too."

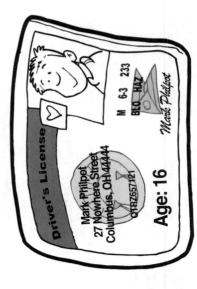

Driver's License

Mark Philpot
27 Nowhere Street
Columbus, OH 44444

QTRZ657121

M 6-3 233
BLO HAZ

Mark Philpot

Age: 16

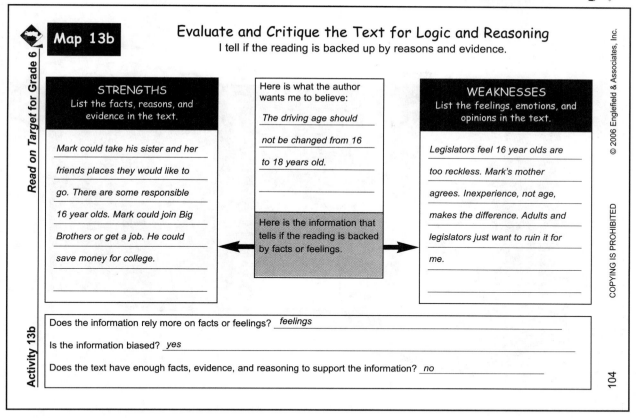

Read on Target for Grade 6

Map 13b

Evaluate and Critique the Text for Logic and Reasoning
I tell if the reading is backed up by reasons and evidence.

STRENGTHS
List the facts, reasons, and evidence in the text.

Mark could take his sister and her friends places they would like to go. There are some responsible 16 year olds. Mark could join Big Brothers or get a job. He could save money for college.

Here is what the author wants me to believe:

The driving age should not be changed from 16 to 18 years old.

Here is the information that tells if the reading is backed by facts or feelings.

WEAKNESSES
List the feelings, emotions, and opinions in the text.

Legislators feel 16 year olds are too reckless. Mark's mother agrees. Inexperience, not age, makes the difference. Adults and legislators just want to ruin it for me.

Activity 13b

Does the information rely more on facts or feelings? *feelings*

Is the information biased? *yes*

Does the text have enough facts, evidence, and reasoning to support the information? *no*

© 2006 Englefield & Associates, Inc.

COPYING IS PROHIBITED

104

Note: Student answers may vary. Example responses in italics are for use as a guide.

Activity 13b   *Read on Target* for Grade 6   103

Step 2

Student Tips

To help you evaluate and critique the text for logic and reasoning, you need to remember:

- Logic and reasoning skills are similar to determining fact and opinion.
- Use the left side of the reading map to list the information that is backed up with facts, reasons, or evidence.
- Use the right side of the reading map to list the information that includes feelings, emotions, or opinions.
- **Completing the chart in the reading map will show you the balance of the argument.**
- This reading map helps you recognize persuasive text and helps you to not be influenced by persuasive feelings. It also helps you recognize texts that are more factual and are backed by reasons and evidence.

Step 3

Complete the reading map. Use the reading map to help you think about evaluating and critiquing for logic and reasoning.

© 2006 Englefield & Associates, Inc.

COPYING IS PROHIBITED

Note: Student answers may vary. Example responses in italics are for use as a guide.

Activity 13b

Step 4

Read the following questions and write your answers.

1. What are the strengths of Mark's argument?

   There are some responsible 16 year olds. If he could drive, Mark could be a Big

   Brother, and he could get a job. If he gets a job, he can save money for college.

2. How do the legislators' opinions differ from Mark's?

   Legislators feel 16 year olds are too reckless; legislators also think 16 year olds

   don't think about the consequences of their actions.

3. When Mark calls his congressman, what do you think he should or should not say?

   Student answers may vary. Mark should explain the benefits of 16 year olds having

   drivers' licenses. These might include part-times jobs, mentor programs, and

   running errands for parents or for siblings.

4. Do you agree with Mark or with the legislators? Why?

   Student answers may vary. I agree with Mark. I think he needs to be able to drive in

   order to go to work. Or, I disagree with Mark. I think the legislators are correct.

   Sixteen year olds are too reckless; they are not responsible.

105

96

Troubleshooting: Evaluating Logic and Reasoning

Looking at writing for logic and reasoning is very similar to the skill of looking for fact and opinion. Students sometimes think if you feel a certain way about something, that makes it true. We need to be sure they understand feelings are opinions with heart.

Using a reading map to sort out what the author has stated that is factual as opposed to what the author has stated that is a feeling will clearly show the student the balance of the argument. A chart listing facts on one side and feelings on the other will graphically demonstrate the weight of the author's argument when a student might otherwise be influenced by heavily persuasive feelings.

It is important to be sure the students focus on the fact column as something that can be proven to be true. Then, they should look at the other ideas in the text and see if they fit in the feeling column. From this visual organization, the students can come to a reasonable conclusion about the validity of the author's argument. They should understand, however, that good persuasive writers often appeal to feelings because they are very powerful persuaders. Emotional appeal does not make an argument weak if there is logic to support the author's position. Using a reading map is a very effective tool to help the student evaluate whether or not the author is simply manipulating the reader or actually has a well-supported thesis.

14 — Evaluate and Critique the Text

Teaching Tips

What Do Students Need to Know?

When students evaluate and critique, they make judgments about how good a story is. Students need to read and to reread a text to decide how successfully the author communicated what he or she wanted to say. Students need to identify the strengths and the weaknesses of nonfictional and fictional information.

Use of the Reading Map

When students evaluate and critique the text, they should discuss the strengths and the weaknesses of the information in the story. Students must reread the strengths and the weaknesses that have been previously identified to answer the questions about the text.

The reading map will guide students to:

- Read the question in the box.

- List the strengths.

- List the weaknesses.

- Write the answer to the question after reviewing the strengths and weaknesses.

Activity 14a   *Read on Target* for Grade 6

Now that George is a grandfather, he continues to help and listen. He listens to young voices telling him important thoughts about how to play dominoes and matching games. He listens to the children's mother when she is concerned about their health and safety. He offers free advice, and it is usually accurate. He helps with his strong arms, tenderly lifting his baby grandchild out of the crib and into his lap while he reads a favorite story in his special way.

I have seen how George demonstrates his kindness and compassion. So many times he has shown his sincerity and genuine concern. He is a man anyone would be proud and lucky to know.

Note: Student answers may vary. Example responses in italics are for use as a guide.

Activity 14a

Evaluate and Critique the Text

I tell about the strengths and weaknesses of what I read.

Step 1

Read the story "George."

George

George is everybody's friend. He never thinks of anyone as a stranger, and he talks to everyone he meets. He talks with people in the grocery store and at the gas station. George is the kind of person who people are attracted to because of his outgoing personality. He is sincere and kind. He is honest and compassionate.

George is about six feet tall with a large body frame accentuated by strong arms and a broad chest. His balding head retains some of the gray, short hair around the sides. In his younger days, his hair was somewhat curly. His hazel eyes are concealed slightly by glasses. His beard is graying to match his hair color, reflective of older age. His beard and hair looked better when they were brown. He looked more like his brother Stephen, but now Stephen's hair is still brown and George's is gray.

All of his life, George has helped others. As a pharmacist, he gave advice to people when they were sick, and he made sure they knew what to do to feel better quickly. He checked to make sure they understood his directions. He assisted people with household tasks, too. He helped carry furniture when people moved. He cleaned up when basements flooded. There was almost no job he wouldn't do. He believed that helping people was important in life.

In addition to helping people, George listened to them. He wanted to hear what they said. He listened to stories about work, and he listened to stories about family life. The more he listened, the more people shared with him. He thought that listening to others showed them what they had to say was important, and he believed it was.

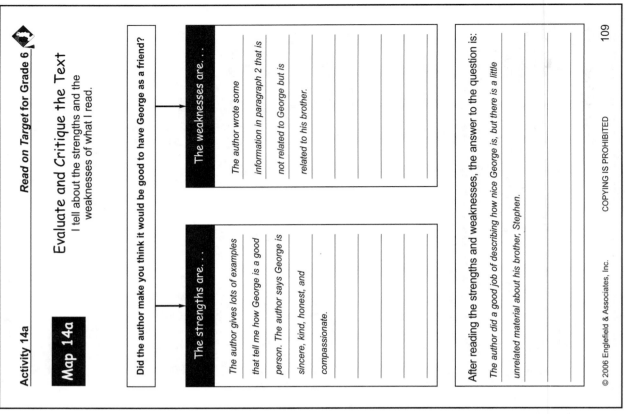

Activity 14a

Evaluate and *Critique* the Text
I tell about the strengths and the weaknesses of what I read.

Map 14a

Did the author make you think it would be good to have George as a friend?

The strengths are. . .

The author gives lots of examples that tell me how George is a good person. The author says George is sincere, kind, honest, and compassionate.

The weaknesses are. . .

The author wrote some information in paragraph 2 that is not related to George but is related to his brother.

After reading the strengths and weaknesses, the answer to the question is:

The author did a good job of describing how nice George is, but there is a little unrelated material about his brother, Stephen.

Note: Student answers may vary. Example responses in italics are for use as a guide.

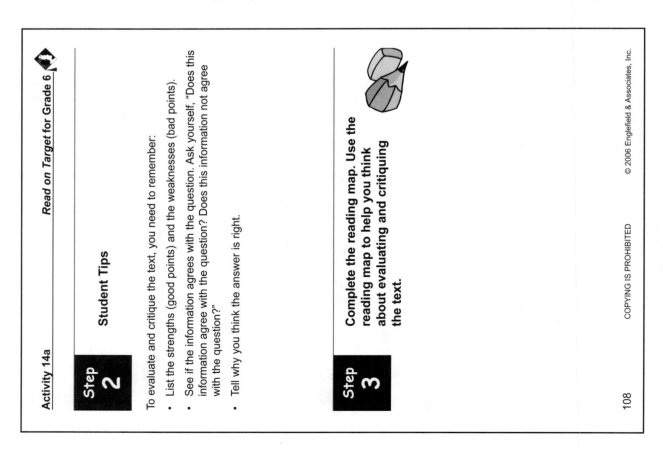

Activity 14a

Step 2   Student Tips

To evaluate and critique the text, you need to remember:

- List the strengths (good points) and the weaknesses (bad points).
- See if the information agrees with the question. Ask yourself, "Does this information agree with the question? Does this information not agree with the question?"
- Tell why you think the answer is right.

Step 3   Complete the reading map. Use the reading map to help you think about evaluating and critiquing the text.

Activity 14b

Evaluate and Critique the Text
I tell about the strengths and weaknesses of what I read.

Step 1   Read the article "The Survey."

The Survey

In this day and age of nutritional awareness regarding calorie intake, types of vitamins, and benefits of food and drink, scientists wanted to find out which types of drinks people preferred. They felt that by providing health and nutrition information, they would influence the preference of people toward a particular type of drink.

As a result, 50 people were given a questionnaire. This form provided information regarding calorie value and health and nutritional information of four different types of drinks. The respondents were asked to rate their preferences for the different types of drinks by rating their favorites. After completion, they were given a coupon to choose one free bottle of diet soda pop, orange juice, regular soda pop, or water. Study the chart on the next page before answering the questions.

111

Note: Student answers may vary. Example responses in italics are for use as a guide.

Step 4   Read the following questions and write your answers.

1. Write one reason why having George as a friend would be good.

Student answers may vary but should include: he talks to everyone he meets, he is

sincere and kind, and he is honest and compassionate.

2. Write another reason why having George as a friend would be good.

Student answers may vary but should include: he talks to everyone he meets, he is

sincere and kind, he is honest and compassionate.

3. Write one reason why having George as a friend would not be good.

George is much older than I am; I'm not sure if we would have many things in

common.

4. Do you think that having George as a friend would be a good idea or a bad idea?

I think having George as a friend would be a good idea. The author gave many

examples that make me believe George would be a good person to be around.

Activity 14b   *Read on Target* for Grade 6

Step 2   Student Tips

To evaluate and critique the text, you need to remember:

- List the strengths (good points) and the weaknesses (bad points).
- See if the information agrees with the question. Ask yourself, "Does this information agree with the question? Does this information not agree with the question?"
- Tell why you think the answer is right.

Step 3   Complete the reading map. Use the reading map to help you think about evaluating and critiquing the text.

© 2006 Englefield & Associates, Inc.   COPYING IS PROHIBITED   113

Activity 14b   *Read on Target* for Grade 6

Type of Drink	Calories per Bottle	Information from the Warnings/Benefits Label	Percent Rated as Favorite Drink
Diet Soda Pop	0	"Great Taste" "Contains Aspartame (some people may be allergic to phenylalanine, an ingredient in aspartame)"	35%
Water	0	"Helps Regulate Body Temperature"	25%
Regular Soda Pop	100	"Tastes Good"	30%
Orange Juice	110	"A Good Source of Vitamin C and Vitamin D" "Great Natural Taste"	10%

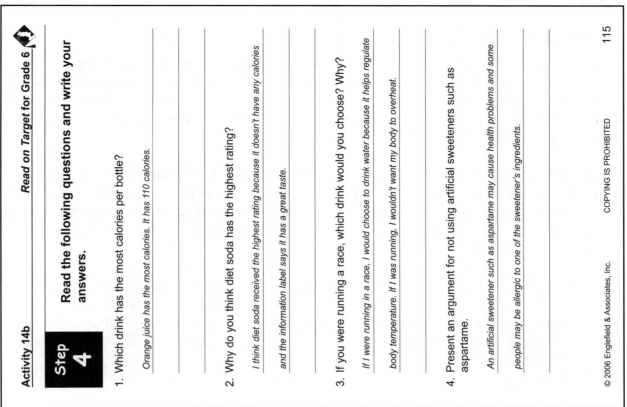

Activity 14b   *Read on Target* for Grade 6

Step 4

Read the following questions and write your answers.

1. Which drink has the most calories per bottle?

   Orange juice has the most calories. It has 110 calories.

2. Why do you think diet soda has the highest rating?

   I think diet soda received the highest rating because it doesn't have any calories and the information label says it has a great taste.

3. If you were running a race, which drink would you choose? Why?

   If I were running in a race, I would choose to drink water because it helps regulate body temperature. If I was running, I wouldn't want my body to overheat.

4. Present an argument for not using artificial sweeteners such as aspartame.

   An artificial sweetener such as aspartame may cause health problems and some people may be allergic to one of the sweetener's ingredients.

© 2006 Englefield & Associates, Inc.   COPYING IS PROHIBITED   115

Note: Student answers may vary. Example responses in italics are for use as a guide.

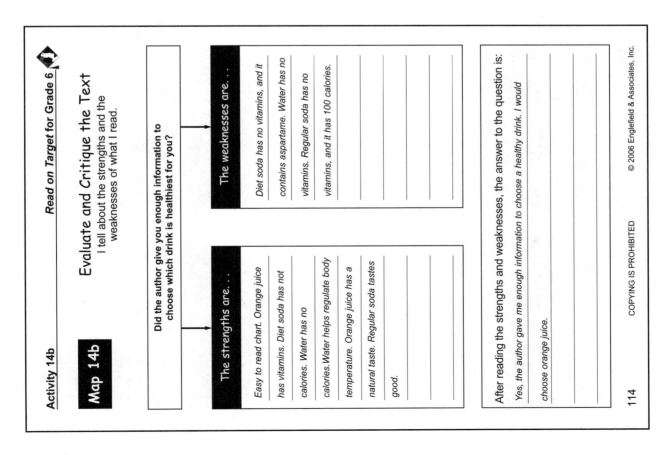

Activity 14b   *Read on Target* for Grade 6

Map 14b

Evaluate and Critique the Text
I tell about the strengths and the weaknesses of what I read.

Did the author give you enough information to choose which drink is healthiest for you?

The weaknesses are. . .

Diet soda has no vitamins, and it contains aspartame. Water has no vitamins. Regular soda has no vitamins, and it has 100 calories.

The strengths are. . .

Easy to read chart. Orange juice has vitamins. Diet soda has not calories. Water has no calories. Water helps regulate body temperature. Orange juice has a natural taste. Regular soda tastes good.

After reading the strengths and weaknesses, the answer to the question is:

Yes, the author gave me enough information to choose a healthy drink. I would choose orange juice.

114   COPYING IS PROHIBITED   © 2006 Englefield & Associates, Inc.

Troubleshooting: Evaluating and Critiquing the Text

Getting students to communicate their opinions regarding reading selections often results in one sentence responses, even when you ask them to include support for their opinions. Students need to read and to reread for pertinent information in order to understand why they have their opinions. They are often unwilling to do this because they do not understand what we are asking them to do.

As teachers, we need to ask specific evaluative questions. For example, the teacher might ask a question such as, "Did the author have a convincing argument that people should be vegetarians?" The student (after class discussion) uses the reading map to go back and to look critically at the text to find strengths and weaknesses in the author's presentation.

The student then has a clear picture as to the answer to the question and has support for his or her opinion. A positive effect of this process is that students begin to perceive the need for thought development in other situations. Another bonus is that, although this is a reading map for evaluating text, it also gives a student a basis for expressing his or her opinions in writing.

15

Summarize the Text

Teaching Tips

What Do Students Need to Know?

A story is summarized when the main idea is restated in the student's own words; details are left out of a summary. Students need to give a brief description of the important information in the story and stay on the topic. A summary is much shorter than what the student reads. Students need to be reminded that in the summary they should have one sentence that tells the overall idea of each paragraph. For example, a summary of four paragraphs generally has one sentence per paragraph. A summary is **not** recopying the text.

Use of the Reading Maps

The reading maps may be used after students have read a paragraph or story. Students that have had little experience in summarizing what they have read may need to begin by reading just one paragraph and crossing out the details in the text. They may need to **highlight** the information that is important. This method will help students distinguish vital information from unnecessary information. Next, students can transfer the important information to the reading map for use in writing a summary sentence.

The reading maps will help students to:

- Circle the **important information** from paragraph 1.

- Rewrite the important information using their **own words** to tell the overall idea of paragraph 1.

- Repeat steps 1 and 2 to include each additional paragraph selected to read.

- Use their **own words** to tell the overall idea of the **whole selection**.

Step 2　Student Tips

To summarize the text you need to remember:

- Each paragraph has a main idea. Tell only the important information in each paragraph. Leave out unimportant information. Use your own words (different words that mean the same thing as the words in the story). Make sure you stay on topic.

- You should follow these steps.

1. Read the whole text.

2. Next, read one paragraph at a time.

3. Circle important information. This will help you know what to write on your reading map.

4. Write one sentence that tells the main idea of each paragraph in your own words.

5. Last, write the overall idea of the whole text in your own words.

Step 3　Complete the reading maps. Use the reading maps to help you think about summarizing the text.

Activity 15a

Summarize the Text

I tell the overall meaning of the story in my own words.

Step 1　Read the article "Beavers of North America."

Beavers of North America

Beavers are furry mammals with teeth that are a distinguishing characteristic. They have two sets of teeth. In front, beavers have four orange-enameled sharp teeth that they use to chop down trees. Beavers also use their teeth to peel bark and cut branches. These front teeth continue to grow and to wear down as the beavers chew and chop wood. In addition to strong front teeth, beavers have 16 teeth in the back of their mouths for chewing. Their teeth help them survive in their environment.

Beavers can be found in North America. Many live in the United States near rivers, streams, ponds, lakes, and woods. They usually weigh about 30 pounds, but some beavers can weigh as much as 70 pounds. An average-sized beaver is approximately 30 inches long. Beavers use their teeth and strong jaw muscles to build lodges and dams. These lodges look like tepee-shaped piles of sticks and logs. The beavers put the sticks and logs together using layers of mud, sticks, and rocks. Because the beaver is a very social animal, several beaver families often occupy a single lodge.

A beaver dam is built near the lodge. The dam makes the water around the lodge deeper so beavers can swim under the lodge to get inside. These ten-foot-long dams can stand as tall as five feet high. They are built from sticks, poles, and solidly packed mud, brush, and stones. As time goes by, repairs are often needed to preserve the strength and effectiveness of the dams.

Beavers are industrious mammals that are interesting to study. The beavers continuously work hard, chopping down new trees to maintain their dams and lodges. They are always busy cutting and building. Perhaps this is why we say a hardworking person is "busy as a beaver."

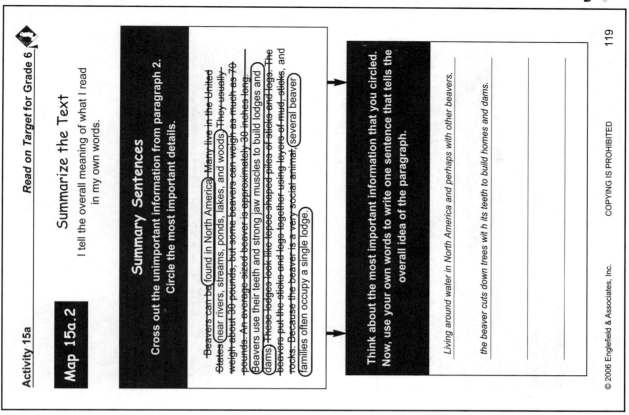

Note: Student answers may vary. Example responses in italics are for use as a guide.

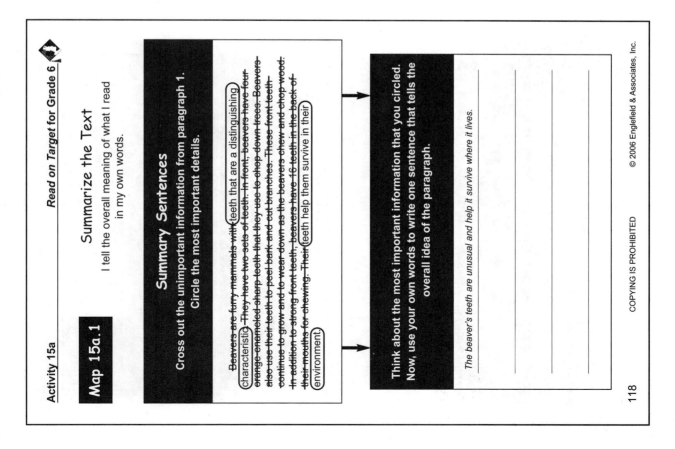

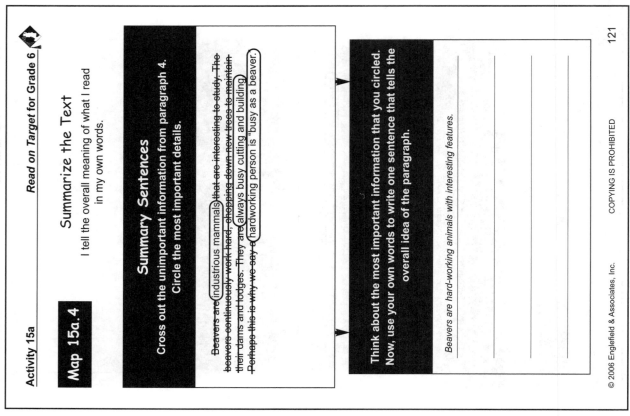

Activity 15a

Read on Target for Grade 6

Summarize the Text

I tell the overall meaning of what I read in my own words.

Map 15a.4

Summary Sentences

Cross out the unimportant information from paragraph 4. Circle the most important details.

Beavers are industrious mammals that are interesting to study. The beavers continuously work hard, chopping down new trees to maintain their dams and lodges. They are always busy cutting and building. Perhaps this is why we say a hardworking person is "busy as a beaver."

Think about the most important information that you circled. Now, use your own words to write one sentence that tells the overall idea of the paragraph.

Beavers are hard-working animals with interesting features.

121

© 2006 Englefield & Associates, Inc.

COPYING IS PROHIBITED

Note: Student answers may vary. Example responses in italics are for use as a guide.

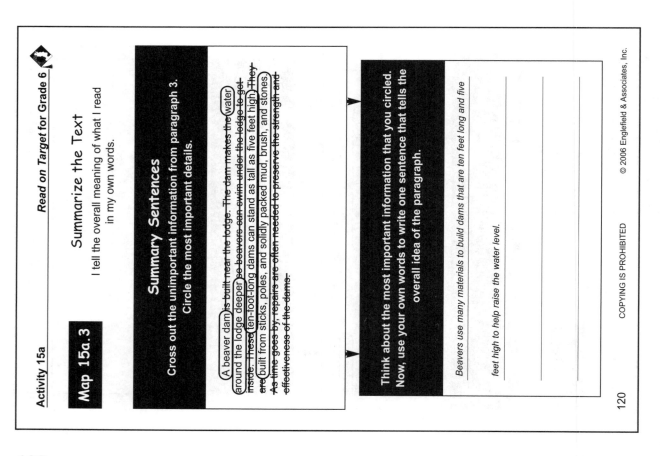

Activity 15a

Read on Target for Grade 6

Summarize the Text

I tell the overall meaning of what I read in my own words.

Map 15a.3

Summary Sentences

Cross out the unimportant information from paragraph 3. Circle the most important details.

A beaver dam is built near the lodge. The dam makes the water around the lodge deeper so beavers can swim under the lodge to get inside. These ten-foot-long dams can stand as tall as five feet high. They are built from sticks, poles, and solidly packed mud, brush, and stones. As time goes by, repairs are often needed to preserve the strength and effectiveness of the dams.

Think about the most important information that you circled. Now, use your own words to write one sentence that tells the overall idea of the paragraph.

Beavers use many materials to build dams that are ten feet long and five

feet high to help raise the water level.

120

© 2006 Englefield & Associates, Inc.

COPYING IS PROHIBITED

COPYING IS PROHIBITED

© 2006 Englefield & Associates, Inc.

Activity 15a   *Read on Target* for Grade 6

Step 4

Read the following questions and write your answers.

1. Write one detail from the first paragraph that tells about beavers' teeth.

   Answers will include one of the following: two sets of teeth, four orange-enameled

   sharp teeth used to chop down trees, use their teeth to peel bark and cut branches,

   front teeth continue to grow and break off as they chew and chop wood, 16 back teeth.

2. Write a summary sentence for the first paragraph.

   The beaver's teeth are unusual and help it survive where it lives.

3. Write a summary sentence for the third paragraph that tells about the beaver dam.

   Beavers use many materials to build dams that are ten feet long and five feet high

   to help raise the water level.

4. Write one sentence to summarize the entire text.

   Beavers are small, hard-working mammals with distinctive teeth used for building

   lodges and dams.

123

Note: Student answers may vary. Example responses in italics are for use as a guide.

Activity 15a   *Read on Target* for Grade 6

Map 15a.5

Summarize the Text
I tell the overall meaning of what I read in my own words.

Use your own words to write one sentence that tells the overall idea of the entire text.

Beavers are small, hard-working mammals with distinctive teeth that they use for

building lodges and dams.

122

Activity 15b

Summarize the Text

I tell the overall meaning of the story in my own words.

Step 1

Read the article "Bottle-Nosed Dolphins."

Bottle-Nosed Dolphins

Bottle-nosed dolphins are sea animals that live in salt water. The name "bottle-nosed" comes from the shape of the animal's snout. The slightly turned-up curve of the mouth, plus the shape of the nose, gives the bottle-nosed dolphin the appearance of always smiling. Many people say they look like friendly pets. In addition to the bottle nose, the unique shape of the dolphin's dorsal fin makes the animal easy to identify.

Bottle-nosed dolphins are marine mammals; that is, they are warm-blooded animals that live in water. Although they swim in waters of varying temperatures, the dolphin's body temperature remains the same. These playful dolphins breathe air through a blowhole on the top of their heads. Like other mammals, baby dolphins drink milk from their mothers. A female dolphin may care for a dolphin calf until it is 18 months old.

Dolphins are intelligent animals. The brains of dolphins and of humans are about the same size. Dolphins navigate through the water by making clicking sounds. When the dolphins send out these high-pitched noises through the water, those sounds bounce off objects in the water. From the echoes, the bottle-nosed dolphin is able to detect the size and location of those objects in the water. Researchers are often interested in studying the dolphin's ability to locate even the smallest object from a far distance.

Marine biologists have learned many things about dolphins by watching them in captivity. There is still much to learn and many questions to answer about these intelligent and friendly-looking mammals.

© 2006 Englefield & Associates, Inc.

Step 2

Student Tips

To summarize the text you need to remember:

- Each paragraph has a main idea. Tell only the important information in each paragraph. Leave out unimportant information. Use your own words (different words that mean the same thing as the words in the story). Make sure you stay on topic.

- You should follow these steps.

1. Read the whole text.

2. Next, read one paragraph at a time.

3. Circle important information. This will help you know what to write on your reading map.

4. Write one sentence that tells the main idea of each paragraph in your own words.

5. Last, write the overall idea of the whole text in your own words.

Step 3

Complete the reading map. Use the reading map to help you think about summarizing the text.

© 2006 Englefield & Associates, Inc.

© 2006 Englefield & Associates, Inc.

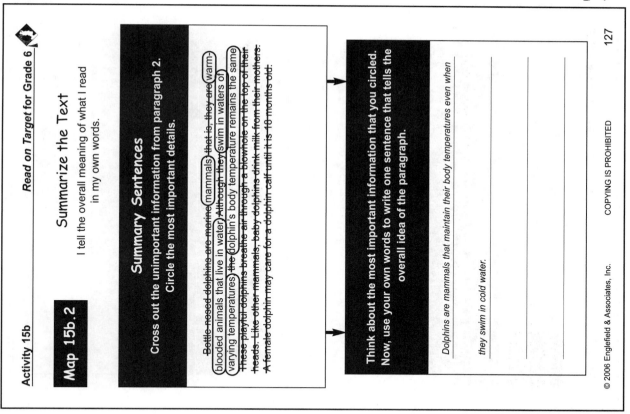

Activity 15b   *Read on Target* **for Grade 6**

Map 15b.2

Summarize the Text

I tell the overall meaning of what I read in my own words.

Summary Sentences

Cross out the unimportant information from paragraph 2. Circle the most important details.

Bottle-nosed dolphins are marine mammals; that is, they are warm-blooded animals that live in water. Although they swim in waters of varying temperatures, the dolphin's body temperature remains the same. These playful dolphins breathe air through a blowhole on the top of their heads. Like other mammals, baby dolphins drink milk from their mothers. A female dolphin may care for a dolphin calf until it is 18 months old.

Think about the most important information that you circled. Now, use your own words to write one sentence that tells the overall idea of the paragraph.

Dolphins are mammals that maintain their body temperatures even when _____

they swim in cold water. _____

127

© 2006 Englefield & Associates, Inc.   COPYING IS PROHIBITED

Note: Student answers may vary. Example responses in italics are for use as a guide.

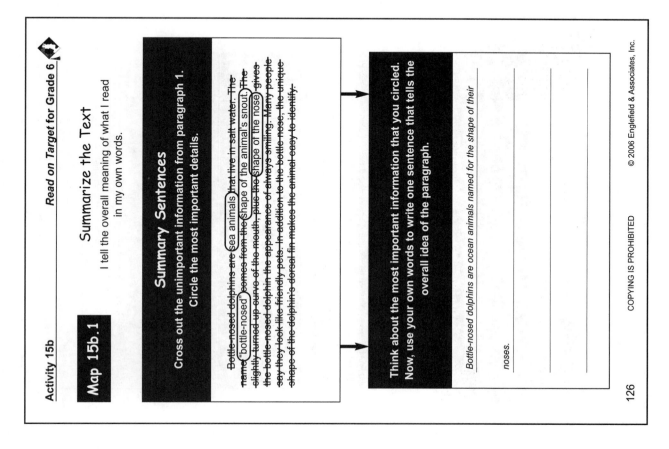

Activity 15b   *Read on Target* **for Grade 6**

Map 15b.1

Summarize the Text

I tell the overall meaning of what I read in my own words.

Summary Sentences

Cross out the unimportant information from paragraph 1. Circle the most important details.

Bottle-nosed dolphins are sea animals that live in salt water. The name "bottle-nosed" comes from the shape of the animal's snout. The slightly turned-up curve of the mouth, plus the shape of the nose, gives the bottle-nosed dolphin the appearance of always smiling. Many people say they look like friendly pets. In addition to the bottle nose, the unique shape of the dolphin's dorsal fin makes the animal easy to identify.

Think about the most important information that you circled. Now, use your own words to write one sentence that tells the overall idea of the paragraph.

Bottle-nosed dolphins are ocean animals named for the shape of their _____

noses. _____

126

COPYING IS PROHIBITED   © 2006 Englefield & Associates, Inc.

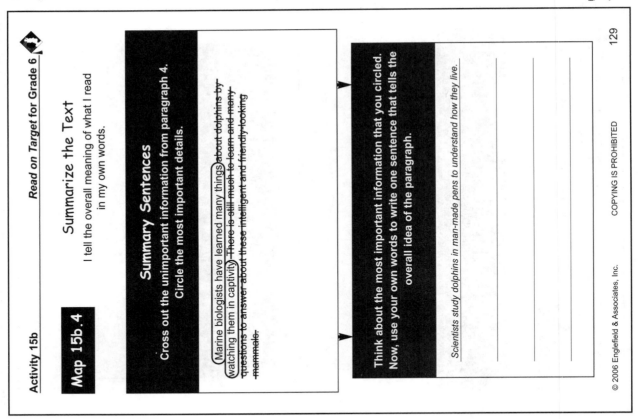

Activity 15b — *Read on Target* for Grade 6

Summarize the Text
I tell the overall meaning of what I read in my own words.

Map 15b.4

Summary Sentences
Cross out the unimportant information from paragraph 4.
Circle the most important details.

(Marine biologists have learned many things) about dolphins by (watching them in captivity). ~~There is still much to learn and many questions to answer about these intelligent and friendly-looking mammals.~~

Think about the most important information that you circled. Now, use your own words to write one sentence that tells the overall idea of the paragraph.

Scientists study dolphins in man-made pens to understand how they live.

129   © 2006 Englefield & Associates, Inc.   COPYING IS PROHIBITED

Note: Student answers may vary. Example responses in italics are for use as a guide.

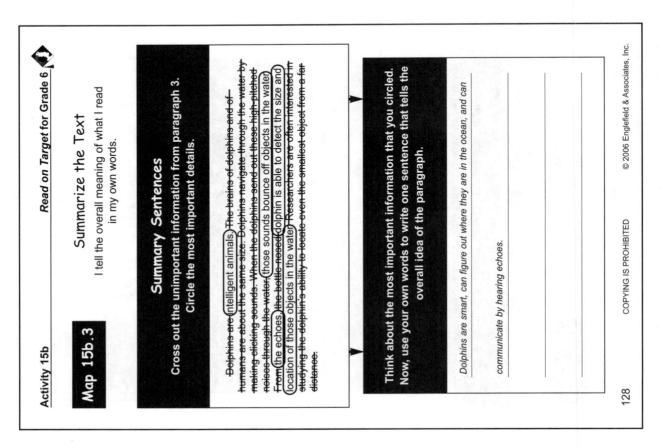

Activity 15b — *Read on Target* for Grade 6

Summarize the Text
I tell the overall meaning of what I read in my own words.

Map 15b.3

Summary Sentences
Cross out the unimportant information from paragraph 3.
Circle the most important details.

~~Dolphins are~~ (intelligent animals.) ~~The brains of dolphins and of humans are about the same size. Dolphins navigate through the water by making clicking sounds. When the dolphins send out these high-pitched noises through the water,~~ (those sounds bounce off objects in the water.) From (the echoes, the bottle-nosed dolphin is able to detect the size and location of those objects in the water.) ~~Researchers are often interested in studying the dolphin's ability to locate even the smallest object from a far distance.~~

Think about the most important information that you circled. Now, use your own words to write one sentence that tells the overall idea of the paragraph.

Dolphins are smart, can figure out where they are in the ocean, and can communicate by hearing echoes.

128   © 2006 Englefield & Associates, Inc.   COPYING IS PROHIBITED

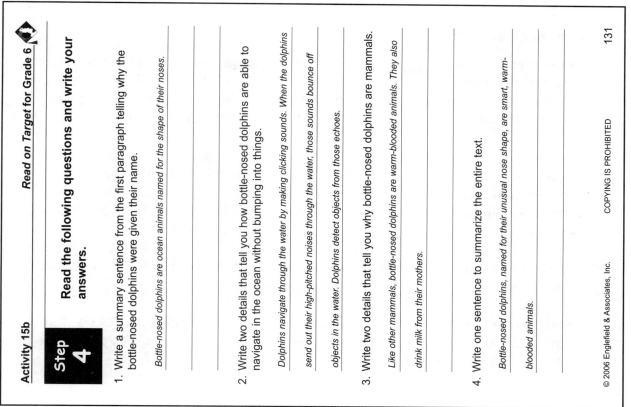

Activity 15b — *Read on Target* for Grade 6

Step 4

Read the following questions and write your answers.

1. Write a summary sentence from the first paragraph telling why the bottle-nosed dolphins were given their name.

   Bottle-nosed dolphins are ocean animals named for the shape of their noses.

2. Write two details that tell you how bottle-nosed dolphins are able to navigate in the ocean without bumping into things.

   Dolphins navigate through the water by making clicking sounds. When the dolphins send out their high-pitched noises through the water, those sounds bounce off objects in the water. Dolphins detect objects from those echoes.

3. Write two details that tell you why bottle-nosed dolphins are mammals.

   Like other mammals, bottle-nosed dolphins are warm-blooded animals. They also drink milk from their mothers.

4. Write one sentence to summarize the entire text.

   Bottle-nosed dolphins, named for their unusual nose shape, are smart, warm-blooded animals.

© 2006 Englefield & Associates, Inc.   COPYING IS PROHIBITED   131

Note: Student answers may vary. Example responses in italics are for use as a guide.

Activity 15b — *Read on Target* for Grade 6

Map 15b.5

Summarize the Text

I tell the overall meaning of what I read in my own words.

Use your own words to write one sentence that tells the overall idea of the entire text.

Bottle-nosed dolphins, named for their unusual nose shape, are smart, warm-blooded animals.

130   COPYING IS PROHIBITED   © 2006 Englefield & Associates, Inc.

Troubleshooting: Summarizing Text

Students sometimes have trouble summarizing because they confuse it with retelling. Summarizing is different from retelling in two very noticeable ways. The first is that in a summary the student needs to recount only the main ideas of the whole selection. The second is that the language in a summary needs to be restated in the student's own words.

A simple way to teach students to summarize is to have students read the whole selection and then reread each paragraph separately, closing the book after each paragraph. Then, in their own words, the students should tell what the main idea of each paragraph is. It is a critical step to read the entire text first so students have a grasp of what the main idea of the whole selection is. Each paragraph becomes one sentence in the summary that states the main idea of the paragraph. The reading map may be modified for the number of paragraphs in the selection.

While reading, the student should be watching for important facts and details that support the main idea that has previously been identified. Following this procedure can be a useful study tool as well as a critical-thinking exercise.

16

Identify Cause and Effect

Teaching Tips

What Do Students Need to Know?

Cause and effect is a critical-thinking skill that requires students to see a relationship between two events. Students need to understand the reason why something happens and what happens as a result. The **cause** is the action or the reason that makes something happen. The **effect** is the result of the cause. A cause can have more than one effect, and an effect can have more than one cause. Vocabulary associated with cause and effect includes: why, what happened, because, since, therefore, as a result, and so.

Use of the Reading Map

To help students determine cause and effect, teachers may write the fill-in-the-blanks statement on the board or overhead. Teachers can emphasize a key word, which signals the relationship and is a clue to figure out the cause and effect. Example:

_____ happened **because** _____.

Effect   Cause

The reading map will guide students to:

- Read the definition of cause and effect and the key words.

- Read the example of a cause and effect statement.

- Write a sentence based on the story that tells the cause (why something happened, the reason or action).

- Write a sentence based on the story that tells the effect (what happened, the result).

Activity 16a

When it is time to land, the air is slowly cooled, and the exact opposite process happens. When the air inside the balloon is cooled, its molecules slow down. They lose energy and take up less space. Cooling the air results in the balloon deflating and losing volume. The air continues to be cooled slowly, so the balloon can sink lower to the ground. Finally, the air is cooled to the point that the balloon contracts. The balloon ride is over as the basket sinks to the ground, but the experience will stay with the balloonists for a long time, all because of hot air!

Activity 16a

Identify Cause and Effect

I read to find out the reason why something happened and what happened.

Step 1   Read the article "A Balloon Ride."

A Balloon Ride

Have you ever wondered how people use a large balloon to fly in the air? It is quite amazing to see a large colorful balloon high up in the sky. Hot air Balloons seem almost magical, but they are really large bags filled with hot air. Balloons have a basket attached so that people can take rides. The baskets are suspended below the balloon. People are able to stand in the basket; they can look around as the balloon lifts off the ground.

You might wonder how the balloon is able to rise with people holding it down. But the hot air behaves in a special way. When air is heated, it warms the air molecules. These molecules start to move faster and faster. The warm molecules push each other and take up more space. As the air continues to heat, the molecules speed up and push harder against each other. The expanded air takes up more space than the cold air. Because the air inside the balloon has expanded, the balloon inflates, increasing in volume.

The hot air that fills the inside of the balloon has fewer molecules than the colder air outside the balloon. Consequently, the hot air weighs less. The balloon rises because the hot air molecules are lighter and weigh less. The balloon pushes up, up, up into the air, high in the sky. As people riding in the basket float up in the sky, they can see many sights below. Farms, houses, trees, and people all seem smaller as the balloon floats away.

Identify Cause and Effect

I read to find out the reason why something happened and what happened.

Map 16a

The air in the balloon takes up more space

Cause: **Why** something happened (Reason/Action)

As a result →

the balloon inflates and increases its volume.

Effect: **What** happened (result)

The balloon rises

Effect: **What** happened (result)

Because →

the hot air is lighter and weighs less.

Cause: **Why** something happened (Reason/Action)

© 2006 Englefield & Associates, Inc.   COPYING IS PROHIBITED   135

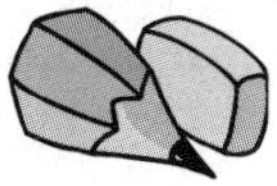

Note: Student answers may vary. Example responses in italics are for use as a guide.

Step 2

Student Tips

To identify cause and effect, you need to remember:

- The **cause** is the action or the reason that makes something happen (why something happened).

- The **effect** is the result (what happened).

- Look for key words that are clues to help you figure out if the statement is a cause or an effect.

- Some of the key words that tell you why something happened (cause) are: **because, since.**

- Some of the key words that tell you what happened (effect) are: **therefore, as a result.**

Example Sentences

Here is an example of a cause and effect sentence:

- **Because** gold was discovered in the west (cause), many people moved to the west to get wealthy (effect).

Sometimes the order is reversed and the effect comes before the cause. Here is an example of an effect and cause sentence:

- Many people moved to the west (effect) **because** gold was discovered (cause).

Step 3

Complete the reading map. Use the reading map to help you think about cause and effect.

134   COPYING IS PROHIBITED   © 2006 Englefield & Associates, Inc.

Activity 16b

Identify Cause and Effect

I read to find out the reason why something happened and what happened.

Step 1   Read the article "Glaciers in Our World."

Glaciers in Our World

Massive, huge, and unusual is how I described the glacier that I saw. As I stood there, shivering underneath my parka, I couldn't believe my eyes. Glaciers are large, ever-drifting masses of ice found in cold regions high in the mountains. The snow builds up quickly, more quickly than it melts. As the snow grows deeper, it compacts and turns to ice.

The glacier I saw was in Switzerland. I spotted it in a valley between two mountains. I think it ranged from 600 feet to 1,000 feet in depth. This valley glacier was extremely thick ice with a long, narrow body that filled high in between the mountains. Its ice was so deep and cold that it appeared deep blue in some spots.

I watched the glacier as our tour guide began to explain how glaciers shaped the land. During the Ice Age, glaciers covered a large part of our world. As glaciers moved across the land, they impacted the land's features, creating a variety of landforms. They were powerful forces, moving and changing the terrain. After the Ice Age was over, the glaciers melted and left behind large holes filled with water. I saw evidence of this as I looked down the mountain; ponds and lake formations were nestled in the mountains, and deposits of bedrock, clay, and sand had been left behind in the valleys.

I couldn't wait to get home. For one thing, I was pretty cold, but I also wanted to do some more research on this amazing natural wonder. I started with an Internet search. I was amazed at the history behind these awesome formations. One of the articles I read said glaciers existed 10,000 years ago. As my tour guide had said, glaciers covered large areas of our world back then.

137   © 2006 Englefield & Associates, Inc.   COPYING IS PROHIBITED

Note: Student answers may vary. Example responses in italics are for use as a guide.

Activity 16a   *Read on Target* **for Grade 6**

Step 4   Read the following questions and write your answers.

1. What causes the balloon to deflate?

   The air is cooled and the molecules slow down. The molecules take less space and lose energy. Cooling the air in the balloon causes the balloon to deflate and to lose volume.

2. Why does the balloon gain volume and expand?

   The balloon gains volume and expands because the molecules are heated, causing them to push hard against each other. The hot air takes up more space than colder air. Heated air speeds up molecules, which causes the balloon to expand.

3. Why does the hot air in the balloon weigh less?

   The hot air has fewer molecules than colder air.

4. If the temperature of the balloon is the same as the air outside of the balloon, what happens to the balloon?

   When the air inside the balloon is the same temperature as the air outside the balloon, the balloon doesn't expand or contract. Therefore, the balloon doesn't rise or fall. The volume of the balloon does not change.

136   COPYING IS PROHIBITED   © 2006 Englefield & Associates, Inc.

Activity 16b   ***Read on Target* for Grade 6**

Step 2   Student Tips

To identify cause and effect, you need to remember:

- The **cause** is the action or the reason that makes something happen (why something happened).

- The **effect** is the result (what happened).

- Look for key words that are clues to help you figure out if the statement is a cause or an effect.

- Some of the key words that tell you why something happened (cause) are: **because, since.**

- Some of the key words that tell you what happened (effect) are: **therefore, as a result.**

<u>Example Sentences</u>

Here is an example of a cause and effect sentence:

- **Because** gold was discovered in the west (cause), many people moved to the west to get wealthy (effect).

Sometimes the order is reversed and the effect comes before the cause. Here is an example of an effect and cause sentence:

- Many people moved to the west (effect) **because** gold was discovered (cause).

Step 3   **Complete the reading map. Use the reading map to help you think about cause and effect.**

© 2006 Englefield & Associates, Inc.   COPYING IS PROHIBITED   139

Activity 16b   ***Read on Target* for Grade 6**

I learned many other interesting facts about glaciers. Glaciers begin to form when the snow falls. In Switzerland, this happens during the long winter in the mountains. In the spring, the snow gradually melts leaving excess water, which refreezes. As you can imagine, the frozen water becomes ice. This ice packs on top of itself. As a result, the ice becomes heavy and compacted, turning into dense crystals of ice. The ice becomes so thick and heavy that it moves under its own pressure. Glaciers are sometimes referred to as "rivers of ice."

How interesting it is to see what happened to our world as a result of glaciers moving across the land! Perhaps you will have an opportunity to study the land formations in your area and discover the effect the glaciers have had.

GLACIER

138   COPYING IS PROHIBITED   © 2006 Englefield & Associates, Inc.

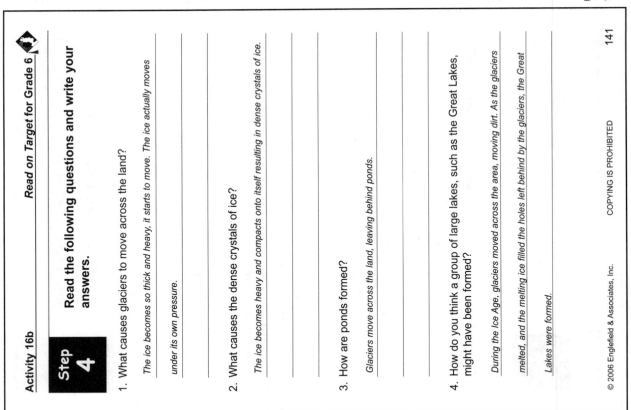

Read on Target for Grade 6

Activity 16b

Step 4

Read the following questions and write your answers.

1. What causes glaciers to move across the land?

   The ice becomes so thick and heavy, it starts to move. The ice actually moves

   under its own pressure.

2. What causes the dense crystals of ice?

   The ice becomes heavy and compacts onto itself resulting in dense crystals of ice.

3. How are ponds formed?

   Glaciers move across the land, leaving behind ponds.

4. How do you think a group of large lakes, such as the Great Lakes, might have been formed?

   During the Ice Age, glaciers moved across the area, moving dirt. As the glaciers

   melted, and the melting ice filled the holes left behind by the glaciers, the Great

   Lakes were formed.

© 2006 Englefield & Associates, Inc.   COPYING IS PROHIBITED

141

Note: Student answers may vary. Example responses in italics are for use as a guide.

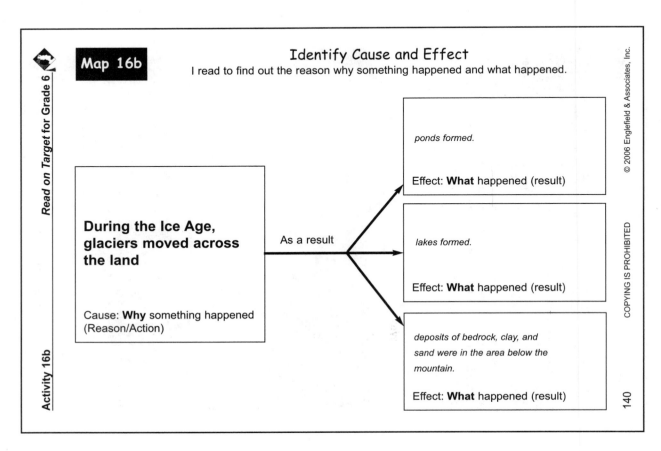

Read on Target for Grade 6

Map 16b

Identify Cause and Effect
I read to find out the reason why something happened and what happened.

During the Ice Age, glaciers moved across the land

Cause: **Why** something happened (Reason/Action)

As a result

ponds formed.

Effect: **What** happened (result)

lakes formed.

Effect: **What** happened (result)

deposits of bedrock, clay, and sand were in the area below the mountain.

Effect: **What** happened (result)

Activity 16b

© 2006 Englefield & Associates, Inc.

COPYING IS PROHIBITED

140

Activity 16c

Step 2　Student Tips

To identify cause and effect, you need to remember:

- The **cause** is the action or the reason that makes something happen (why something happened).

- The **effect** is the result (what happened).

- Look for key words that are clues to help you figure out if the statement is a cause or an effect.

  - Some of the key words that tell you why something happened (cause) are: **because, since.**

  - Some of the key words that tell you what happened (effect) are: **therefore, as a result.**

<u>Example Sentences</u>

Here is an example of a cause and effect sentence:

- **Because** gold was discovered in the west (cause), many people moved to the west to get wealthy (effect).

Sometimes the order is reversed and the effect comes before the cause. Here is an example of an effect and cause sentence:

- Many people moved to the west (effect) **because** gold was discovered (cause).

Step 3　**Complete the reading map. Use the reading map to help you think about cause and effect.**

© 2006 Englefield & Associates, Inc.　　　　COPYING IS PROHIBITED

143

Activity 16c

Identify Cause and Effect

I read to find out the reason why something happened and what happened.

Step 1　**Read the article "The Biggest Wave."**

The Biggest Wave

Every so often, incredibly huge waves move in the ocean. They have enormous speed and intensity. These immense, swift-moving waves are called tidal waves or tsunamis. Tsunamis are more common in the Pacific Ocean than anywhere else on Earth.

Scientists are researching the causes of tsunamis. They have found that tsunamis can be the result of a sudden drop in part of the ocean floor. They can also be caused by underwater landslides or earthquakes. Such land movements under the ocean can cause a tremendous underwater wave. At first, the wave looks like a small ripple. However, the wave gains power and force as it continues toward the shore. It then becomes a dangerous, fast-moving wave of lightning speed and unimaginable power.

Many people have seen incredible destruction brought about by this dangerous tidal wave. As the waves go barreling to the shore, they crash into anything in their way. Tsunamis can smash houses, trees, and anything else in their paths.

Since scientists have no way of knowing how often an underwater disturbance that could create a tsunami will occur, it is important to start mapping the floor of the ocean. The ocean floor is covered with underwater mountains and trenches. Earthquakes, landslides, and other sudden drops of the ocean floor are important events that scientists are working hard to discover more about. As scientists conduct research into the causes of tsunamis, they should be able to predict the occurrence of these tidal waves. That way, people can be warned, find safety, and protect their belongings before the tsunamis arrive.

142　　COPYING IS PROHIBITED　　　　© 2006 Englefield & Associates, Inc.

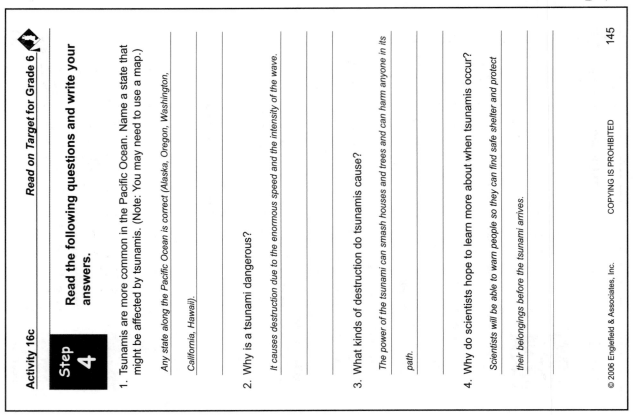

Activity 16c   ***Read on Target* for Grade 6**

Step 4

Read the following questions and write your answers.

1. Tsunamis are more common in the Pacific Ocean. Name a state that might be affected by tsunamis. (Note: You may need to use a map.)

Any state along the Pacific Ocean is correct (Alaska, Oregon, Washington, California, Hawaii).

2. Why is a tsunami dangerous?

It causes destruction due to the enormous speed and the intensity of the wave.

3. What kinds of destruction do tsunamis cause?

The power of the tsunami can smash houses and trees and can harm anyone in its path.

4. Why do scientists hope to learn more about when tsunamis occur?

Scientists will be able to warn people so they can find safe shelter and protect their belongings before the tsunami arrives.

© 2006 Englefield & Associates, Inc.   COPYING IS PROHIBITED   145

Note: Student answers may vary. Example responses in italics are for use as a guide.

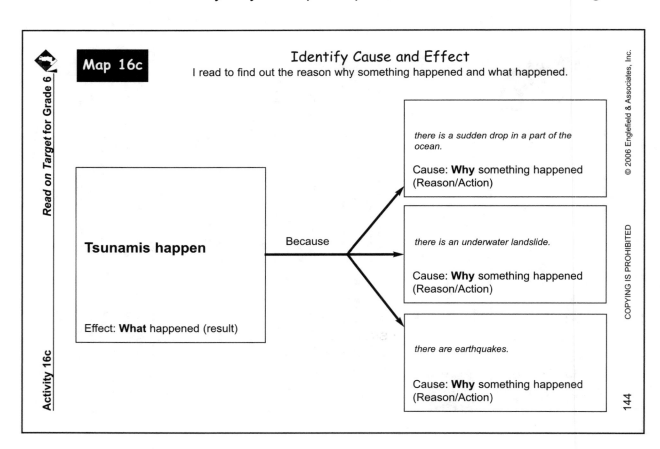

Map 16c

Identify Cause and Effect
I read to find out the reason why something happened and what happened.

Tsunamis happen

Effect: **What** happened (result)

Because →

there is a sudden drop in a part of the ocean.
Cause: **Why** something happened (Reason/Action)

there is an underwater landslide.
Cause: **Why** something happened (Reason/Action)

there are earthquakes.
Cause: **Why** something happened (Reason/Action)

Activity 16c   ***Read on Target* for Grade 6**

© 2006 Englefield & Associates, Inc.   COPYING IS PROHIBITED   144

Troubleshooting: Cause and Effect

If a student is reading a nonfiction piece using cause and effect order, it becomes very complex because there are several logical ways to organize cause and effect. Cause and effect order links what happens to why something happens, and it is rarely a simple "because of this, that" situation. There are usually multiple parts to cause/effect relationships. Students need to see this because if we, as teachers, say there is only one way to write cause and effect, we are going to impair students' abilities to see the logic.

For example, an author might choose to start with the causes of the Civil War and work into the effect. Another author might choose to show how a chain of cause and effect incidents led to the rise of literacy in the Middle Ages. Another author could choose to begin with the effect and work back through the causes. In any case, **your explanation will be much stronger with reading maps that help students to visualize your lesson**. There can be multiple causes and effects, and the order can vary. Teachers may need to use the cause and effect reading maps to provide additional direction for students in conjunction with the Evaluate and Critique for Organizational Structure reading map.

Here are some examples of how cause and effect can vary.

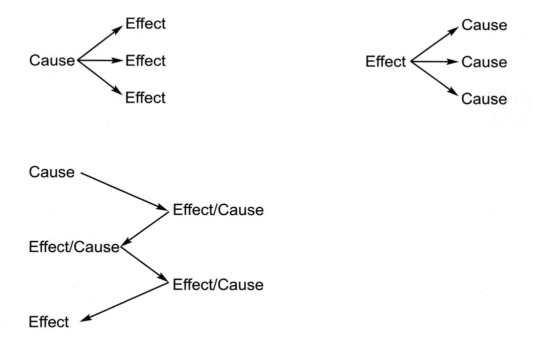

The most important element for students to see when evaluating cause and effect order is that the author has clearly stated the cause and effect relationship regardless of the path he or she takes. There should be clear connections between cause and effect with the use of clue words that show cause and effect (because, therefore, as a result, etc). There is an apparent logical order, and there are ample facts or details to support the cause and effect relationship.

Chapter 5:
Conclusion

Concluding Remarks

Incorporating new instructional techniques is exciting for parents and teachers of all grades and subjects. Critical-thinking skills are a vital part of instruction and assessment in the classroom and can easily be incorporated into the content of reading. Students do not always know how to respond to questions requiring critical-thinking skills. Teachers and parents can guide students toward understanding the requirements of critical thinking by using the sequential instructional process outlined in the designing instruction section. This instructional process will reinforce the strengths of instruction currently in use and support modifications, if necessary, to enhance overall instruction.

Read on Target provides a visual tool for teachers and parents to assist students when answering critical-thinking-skill questions. *Read on Target* contains reading maps that can be used in all content areas to enhance reading comprehension. In addition, teacher tips and troubleshooting pages provide valuable insight into the complexities of each critical-thinking skill. Teachers and parents are aware of the need for continued, repeated practice for students in order to correctly respond to critical-thinking-skill questions. *Read on Target* provides teachers and parents an easy-to-use method for daily practice and reinforcement of critical-thinking skills.

Read on Target is the answer to an educator's search for help in teaching critical-thinking skills. It offers a visual format both in the form of reading maps and designing instruction, and practical information for troubleshooting instructional problems in the classroom. Some texts have limited exposure or explanation of critical-thinking skills. Consequently, students may experience infrequent opportunities to practice these skills in a structured, organized, and clearly stated manner. This can result in reduced intensity and duration of instruction for students who need more than cursory exposure. Using *Read on Target* will focus instruction and assist in the preparation of materials for students to adequately respond to critical-thinking questions. *Read on Target* is a unique resource that teaches how to design instruction to meet student needs, provides organized reading maps to enhance reading comprehension, and clearly states expectations for skills associated with critical thinking.

Additional Resources

Reading Book List for Grade 6

The following titles can be used as texts for the critical-thinking elements. Each text can be matched with a specific reading map for an additional reading comprehension lesson. The list of titles is categorized by fiction, poetry, and nonfiction. This list is not meant to be comprehensive, and additional texts may be used to support your lessons.

Fiction:

Armstrong, William	*Sounder*
Bradford, Emma	*Kat and the Missing Notebooks*
Eager, Edward	*The Well-Wishers*
English, Karen	*Francie*
Farley, Walter	*The Black Stallion Mystery*
Farley, Steven	*The Yearling*
Gipson, Fred	*Old Yeller*
Gipson, Fred	*Savage Sam*
Manes, Stephen	*Be a Perfect Person in Just Three Days!*
Martin, Ann M.	The Baby-Sitters Club Series
MacLachlan, Patricia	*Sarah, Plain and Tall*
Rawls, Wilson	*Where the Red Fern Grows*
Sachar, Louis	*Holes*
Van Draanen, Wendelin	*Sammy Keyes Mystery Series*
White, E.B.	*The Trumpet of the Swan*
White, E.B.	*Charlotte's Web*
White, E.B.	*Stuart Little*
Wilder, Laura Ingalls	The Little House Series

Poetry:

selected by Myra Cohn Livingston	*Lots of Limericks*
Moss, Jeff	*The Butterfly Jar*
Moss, Jeff	*The Other Side of the Door*
Prelutsky, Jack	*A Pizza The Size of The Sun*
Prelutsky, Jack	*The New Kid on The Block*
Prelutsky, Jack	*The Beauty of the Beast: Poems from the Animal Kingdom*
Prelutsky, Jack	*For Laughing Out Loud: Poems to Tickle Your Funny Bone*
Prelutsky, Jack	*Poems of A. Nonny Mouse*
Prelutsky, Jack	*The Pack Rat's Day and Other Poems*
Prelutsky, Jack	*Something Big Has Been Here*
Silverstein, Shel	*Where the Sidewalk Ends*
Silverstein, Shel	*A Light in the Attic*
Silverstein, Shel	*Falling Up*
Silverstein, Shel	*The Missing Piece*
Untermeyer, Louis (editor)	*Rainbow in the Sky*

Nonfiction:

Ardley, Neil   *How Things Work*

Burnie, David   *Eyewitness: Life*

Charley, Catherine   *Tombs and Treasures*

Collins, David R.   *Arthur Ashe: Against the Wind*

Conklin, Thomas   *The Titanic Sinks!*

Couper, Heather and Nigel Henbest   *How the Universe Works*

Fisher, Maxine   *Walt Disney*

Freedman, Russell   *Eleanor Roosevelt: A Life of Discovery*

Lowry, Lois   *Looking Back: A Book of Memories*

Lincoln/Holzer   *Abraham Lincoln, The Writer*

Little, Jean   *Little By Little: A Writer's Education*

Nardo, Don   *Franklin D. Roosevelt*

Knapp, Ron   *Charles Barkley Star Forward*

Krohn, Katherine   *Princess Diana*

Meyer, Susan E.   *Edgar Degas (First Impressions)*

Old, Wendie C.   *The Wright Brothers: Inventors of the Airplane*

Parr, Jan   *Amelia Earhart: First Lady of Flight*

Peet, Bill   *Bill Peet: An Autobiography*

Potter, Joan and Constance Clayton   *African Americans Who Were First*

Roberston, Jr., James I.   *Civil War!: America Become One Nation*

Scholastic   *The Kids Book of the 50 Great States*

Stine, R.L.   *It Came From Ohio: My Life as a Writer*

Time-Life Books   *Our Environment*

Wu, Norbert   *Life in the Oceans*

Yue, Charlotte and David   *The Pueblo*

Student Self-Scoring Chart

Teachers should have students rate how well they understand the critical-thinking steps by putting a star (★) for mastery, a plus sign (+) for making progress, and a minus sign (−) for needs help. Students can rate themselves at the end of each grading period.

Characters	1	2	3	4
Name a character				
Match sentences with the descriptions of the character				
Tell how the character impacts the story				
Tell how the story would be different if you changed a characteristic of the character				

Setting	1	2	3	4
Describe the setting: Tell where the story takes place				
Describe the setting: Tell when the story takes place				
Describe the setting: Tell what the setting looks like				
Tell how the setting affects the characters				
Tell how the setting affects the events				
Change the setting: Change where the story takes place				
Change the setting: Change when the story takes place				
Change the setting: Change what the setting looks like				
Tell how the characters would be different if the setting changed				
Tell how the events would be different if the setting changed				

Plot	1	2	3	4
Describe the chain of events by writing the major events in correct order				
Change the plot by choosing an event to happen earlier or later				
Tell how the story is different when one of the events has been changed				
Take an event out of the story				
Tell what would be different if one of the events is left out of the story				
Write what would happen if the character's actions were different				

Problem/Solution	1	2	3	4
Know the definition of a problem and a solution				
Write the problem of the story you read				
Write the events that lead up to the solution				
Write the solution of the story				
Write a different problem by making up your own problem				
Write how the events would be different if the problem changed				
Write how the solution would be different if the problem changed				

Point of View	1	2	3	4
Know the definition and key word pronouns of each point of view				
Identify the point of view in the story				
Write sentences from the story that helped you figure out the point of view				
Tell why the author writes from the point of view				
Tell how changing the point of view would affect the story				

Theme	1	2	3	4
Name some ideas from the text that tell what the story is about				
Write the lessons that the character learned				
Write a sentence telling what the message of the story is				

Infer	1	2	3	4
Read each sentence/paragraph to find clues about the story's meaning				
Write a clue in the clue box				
Write about an experience or knowledge you have of a similar thing				
Put the clue and your experience or knowledge together to make an inference about what is happening in the story				
Read more of the story to see if the inference is correct				

Predict	1	2	3	4
Read each sentence/paragraph to find clues about the story's meaning				
Write a clue in the clue box				
Write about an experience or knowledge you have of a similar thing				
Put the clue and your experience or knowledge together to make a prediction about what will happen next				
Read more of the story to see if the prediction is correct				

Compare and Contrast	1	2	3	4
Write the names of the things to be compared and contrasted				
Describe the characteristics				
If the items have same characteristics, mark them with a plus sign				
If the items have different characteristics, mark them with a minus sign				

Fact and Opinion	1	2	3	4
Write sentences that tell you if the text is a fact or an opinion				
Write how the information can be proven by evidence or observation				
Write where you would look up information to check it				
Tell if the information is true for everyone				
Write key words that are clues to tell how someone thinks or feels				
Write how the information tells a personal belief or judgment				
Tell if the information is true for some people				

Explain Purpose for Writing	1	2	3	4
Know the definitions and purposes of fiction, poetry, and nonfiction				
Identify the type of writing				
Write the author's purpose				
Write a sentence or sentences from the story that show an example of the author's purpose				

COPYING IS PROHIBITED   © 2006 Englefield & Associates, Inc.

	1	2	3	4
Evaluate and Critique the Text for Organizational Structure				
Know the definitions of the types of organizational structure				
Write the types of organizational structure used				
List some ways the organization is a strength or a weakness				
Write how effective the organization is and why				

	1	2	3	4
Evaluate and Critique the Text for Logic and Reasoning				
Write what the author wants you to think or believe				
List the sentences that contain facts, reasons, or evidence				
List the sentences that contain feelings, emotions, or opinions				
Determine if the information if biased				
Determine if the information has enough evidence to support the author's belief				

	1	2	3	4
Evaluate and Critique the Text				
Read the question given by the teacher				
List the strengths of the text				
List the weaknesses of the text				
After reading the strengths and weaknesses, answer the question				

	1	2	3	4
Summarize the Text				
Circle the important information from each paragraph				
Rewrite the important information in each paragraph using your own words				
Use your own words to tell the overall idea of the whole selection				

	1	2	3	4
Identify Cause and Effect				
Know the definitions of cause and effect				
Read the key words for cause and effect				
Write why something happened (the cause)				
Write what happened (the effect)				

<u>Teacher Notes</u>

Teacher Notes

Subject-Specific Skill Development
Workbooks Increase Testing Skills

**Write on Target
for grades 1/2,
3, 4, 5, and 6**

**Includes
Graphic Organizers**

**Read on Target
for grades 1/2,
3, 4, 5, and 6**

**Includes
Reading Maps**

Math on Target for grades 3, 4, and 5

Includes Thinking Maps

For more information, call our toll-free number: 1.877.PASSING (727.7464)
or visit our website: www.showwhatyouknowpublishing.com